novum premium

The Reason

Life, an unpredicted journey between struggle and prosperity

by
Regina Ioannou-Knapp

novum premium

www.novumpublishing.com

All rights of distribution, including via film, radio, and television, photomechanical reproduction, audio storage media, electronic data storage media, and the reprinting of portions of text, are reserved.

© 2019 novum publishing

ISBN 978-1-64268-004-1
Edited by Ioannou Family
Cover photo:
Sotiris Ioannou Photography
Cover design, layout & typesetting:
novum publishing

www.novumpublishing.com

Contents

PROLOGUE
Autopilot 11

PART ONE
Austria 17
Paris 23
Passing of my parents 41
Cyprus 59
Year 1987. 74

PART TWO
February 2002 85
Innocence 93
Motherhood 105
Earthly Angel 131
Invisible 144
Control 151
Jealousy 165
Forgive 176

PART THREE
Tradition 180
Why? 188
Year 2013. 196

AFTERWORD
My Learnings 200

For my beloved husband

Some names and personal details have been changed to protect the identities of those individuals.

A woman is like a tea bag –
You can't tell how strong she is until you put her in hot water.

Eleanor Roosevelt

My gratitude to my beloved children

This book wouldn't exist as such without the loving and supportive participation of my five children. At my 60th birthday, I received a letter from them with the following words:

Dear Mother,

Now is time for you! It's time to write your story, which we are certain that will be a meaningful and unique one, a woman can share. You have succeeded so brilliantly in all your tasks, not only you have been such a loving and caring mother, but also, you were a role model for all the people who have crossed your path. You have given us all the love a mother and father can give to their children which has made us grow strong and healthy. You were always there when we needed you most.

We thank you from the bottom of our hearts.

Your Children,
Markos, Eva, Diogenis, Adonis Jr. and Cleopatra

PROLOGUE

Autopilot. Have you ever experienced that feeling of being on autopilot? Or more specifically, do you know the feeling of having been on autopilot? Have you ever arrived somewhere, in your car or on foot, a journey you have done a thousand times, and stood there at your destination, thinking; *I have absolutely no memory of getting here*? Did the car drive itself? Was I sleepwalking? The moment you become aware of your surroundings, it feels as if you've been jolted awake, as if you're suddenly catching up with the real world, coming crashing back into real time, after a brief spell in another dimension. The point is, when you're on autopilot you're not conscious of what's happening, but as soon as you come out of it, you realize you must have followed your usual routine without noticing it because you have, actually, ended up where you were supposed to be.

This is exactly how I felt as I "woke up" to find myself sitting in my car, parked in a layby off the main highway between Paphos and Limassol, on the south coast of Cyprus. *How did I get here?* I asked myself. It was where I was meant to be, where I came every morning at the time, after the school run and before I went to work, but that day I simply didn't remember anything leading up to that moment.

I searched my memory. Had I completed my usual morning routine? Had I definitely taken the children to school that morning or had I forgotten and left them at home? I couldn't even remember having seen them. What were they wearing? What had we talked about? I felt as if I had just been a million miles away from my own being, and yet here I was, sitting exactly where I always sat at this exact time every morning, in my car, parked up along the coastal road, level with Petra tou Romiou (a rock stack, also known as "Aphrodite's Rock" or "Rock of Aphrodite"), about to go for my morning swim. This was part of my daily routine; a simple ritual that was keeping me attached to my sanity by the thinnest thread, as I struggled through the hardest years of my life.

Every morning I would take my two youngest children, Adonis Jr. and Cleopatra, to their new secondary school in Limassol, which was a 40-minute drive from our house. On the way back, I would stop off at this stunning spot to regain my senses and re-energize myself before going to work. I would park the car, cross the road, step over the low barrier and climb down the rocks to the pebbly beach. I would leave my clothes on a rock and go for a brief swim in the sea, which was always calm at this time in the morning; the tide didn't wake up and gather any real strength until after 9 a.m.

On this particular morning, I took extra care as I climbed down the rocks; I felt a little shaky after my autopilot experience. It hadn't surprised me; it wasn't the first time I had experienced the sensation of virtually losing consciousness whilst going through the motions of my usual routine. My mind was completely and constantly preoccupied with fear at that time; I was almost buckling under the stress, so it was no wonder why I blanked out sometimes. I was scared out of my mind about what the future held for my family; it seemed as though a number of people were determined to destroy us and I didn't know how to fight them off. At this point, I believed there was really no one I could turn to for help. I was living moment to moment, focusing on each new task as it came up, just trying to survive, clinging on to my daily routine. I had been operating like this for a few years by this point and, although I was terrified of admitting it, I knew I was close to breaking point. What I had just experienced had really frightened me. I've had these "autopilot" experiences a few times before, but never for as long as this one. I literally had no memory of the whole morning. The last thing I could remember was some point the previous evening. I was desperate; I was at rock bottom.

As I stripped off my dress and walked out into the shallow waters in my bathing suit, I thought about the first time I ever heard the term "autopilot."

In August 1973, when I was 21 and living in Paris, I did a three-month English language course in London. On the way there, I had taken a boat across the channel, however, my biggest dream was to take a flight back from London to Paris. After studying hard during the daytime and working long hours as a janitor in Saint Mary's Hospital in Paddington during the nighttime, sweeping floors and preparing breakfast for the following morning, I had managed to save up enough money to take a flight back to Paris. It was to be my first ever experience in an airplane.

With no idea what to expect, I took a bus to Heathrow Airport and checked my suitcase in at the Air France desk. My boarding card showed that I was in the seat 10A, which I assumed, correctly, was a window seat. I was filled with excitement as I waited to board the airplane; I had heard so much about this glamorous form of travel and could hardly believe it was my turn to experience it.

I took my seat and found myself sitting beside a French businessman; who was busy writing in his notebook. He must have so much experience with air travel, I thought to myself, to be so comfortable and relaxed that he can turn his attention to something else. By contrast, I couldn't possibly think of or do anything but focus on the new sights and sounds around me. I hadn't slept much the night before; I had been too excited to sleep. I was going to be the first member of my family to experience air travel; I couldn't wait!

I watched the stewardesses showing people to their seats and putting bags in the overhead compartments, thinking to myself, how on earth can this machine get into the air with so many people and bags inside it, it must weigh thousands of kilos, how can it possibly leave the ground? I looked out of the window at the huge wings and engines. My stomach was in a tight knot; I was suddenly extremely nervous.

As I turned to look around the cabin again, I noticed a stewardess opening the cockpit door. I sat up in my seat to get a good look at what was beyond the door and saw two men. Assuming these were the pilots, in my ignorance I wondered why it took two men to fly an airplane when it only took one person to drive a car. Another stewardess was now walking down the aisle offering drinks and newspapers. I didn't take anything offered to me for fear I would have to pay for them. I had saved up and spent every spare penny I had to buy this airplane ticket, so I had nothing left for any unnecessary purchases.

I watched anxiously as another stewardess closed the doors and started explaining all the safety instructions to the passengers, pointing out the emergency exits. This was a little alarming. I had never seen a safety demonstration on a boat or a bus! Perhaps flying is not so safe after all, I thought to myself; maybe I should have taken the boat back instead. I began to have second thoughts about my decision, but it was a little too late to change my mind, as the airplane was already pushing back from the gate. We began traveling slowly towards the runway, and I watched out of the window as we passed many stationary airplanes that were still being loaded up with their cargo. Finally, we made a wide turn and accelerated so quickly that I was forced back into my seat abruptly. We raced down the runway, traveling faster and faster, until I felt the airplane was about to take-off. I felt a heavy pressure on my chest that pinned me back in my seat. The airplane's nose tilted more steeply, and with another sudden jolt, I realised that we had left the ground. I watched out of the window as the land fell away and the objects on it grew smaller and smaller; it was terrifying and exhilarating all at the same time.

After a few more minutes, I felt and heard a tremendous crunch coming from below. Petrified, I looked down and gasped, thinking something must have gone wrong. I was convinced we were going to have to turn back and land. My neighbouring seatmate must have noticed my distress and he leaned over to assure me that everything was fine. He explained that it was just the landing gear being pulled up and stowed away inside the belly of the airplane.

When I told him that I was experiencing flying for the first time, he started to explain in more detail how the airplane worked.

He also told me that the refreshments and newspapers were complimentary, so when the stewardess next came around, I accepted a coffee. My new friend took it upon himself to ask the stewardess if it would be possible for me to go and see the cockpit. She said she would take me as soon as she had finished serving drinks.

I had never felt so excited in my life as I followed the stewardess through that tiny door into what looked like a scene from a science fiction movie. I found myself in an alien world full of flashing lights, instruments, dials and levers. I looked past the cockpit panel and through the big, sloping windows at the endless expanse of azure blue sky all around us.

The pilot and co-pilot greeted me with charming smiles and started to explain how the airplane worked. After a minute or so, I interrupted them to confess my growing concern that they were not holding any of the controls. This was when they explained the concept of the *autopilot* to me. Even though these pilots assured me that an airplane could stay up in the air and on course because of a computerised navigation system program, still for many years it seemed such an implausible concept to me.

Finally, on the island of Cyprus, more than 30 years later, I understood what it meant to be on "autopilot." Autopilot, I discovered, is when your body goes through a preprogrammed routine while your conscious mind is somewhere else entirely.

Once I was waist-deep in the water, I started to swim. After a couple of minutes, I turned over and floated on my back for a moment, looking up at that same azure blue sky I had marveled at through the cockpit windows of that airplane. I thought about the incredible beauty of the natural world and felt what a privilege it was to be present in it. My thoughts kept returning to that first ever flight I took from London to Paris. That safety demonstration had alarmed me at the time, but since then, with all the flights I had taken due to my career in the travel industry, I had seen the same demonstration hundreds of times. I know it so well that I barely pay any attention to it these days. I thought of the countless times I had seen cabin crew pointing out those emergency exits. Where were my emergency exits now? Why doesn't life have an oxygen mask that drops down when you're gasping for breath? Put your own mask on first and then attend to the children, they tell you. You can't save the children if you are suffocating yourself, they tell you. What was I doing? Was I saving myself first? Or was I drowning?

I remained perfectly still, floating on my back, slowly drifting out to the sea. Suddenly, I wished I could keep on drifting. I wanted to float all the way out, away from everything, where no one could find me. But I knew I had to go back.

I turned my body upright and started to tread water. I looked back at the shore, and at the beautiful rock formation, Aphrodite's Rock, that meant so much to me. I looked at Cyprus, thinking about everything that had brought me here. Then, impulsively, I inhaled deeply, held my breath, closed my eyes and ducked my head down so that my whole body was submerged in the sea. I immediately felt safe, immersed in the magical Mediterranean Sea. I curled myself up into a ball and for a moment wished, with all my heart, that I could stay in that peaceful place forever, not breathing, not hearing, not looking, not doing anything, just floating in a fetal position—weightless, suspended in the cool water. I felt such relief I actually wondered how I was going to find the strength to raise my head above the water again.

Save yourself first, I remembered..., so you can save the children.

PART ONE

Austria. I was born in May 1952 in Austria, the middle child of three; my brother was born two years before me, and my sister two years after me. We lived in the upper regions of the Tyrolean Mountains, above the village of Kirchdorf, which is not too far from the town of Kitzbühel, in the lower part of Tyrol. The area is famous for its extraordinary panoramic views of the year-round snow-capped peaks of the Kitzbühel Alps.

When I was a young child, aside from our weekly obligatory church visit to Sunday mass in the village, we rarely left the beautiful, natural countryside that surrounded our house. We lived in the heart of the rural Austrian countryside, where farmers grazed their cattle during the summer months. We lived in a traditional wooden Tyrolean house, much like a Swiss chalet, surrounded by the steep mountain pastures. The ground floor was built from handmade bricks and the first floor was made entirely of wood. Large verandas, over which the wooden roof extended, encircled the first floor of the house.

After mass on Sunday, we would do our weekly shopping at the nearby grocers, which sold just about everything you could think of. The same shop served as the village bank, the post office and the petrol station; it really was a one-stop shop!

My parents were farmers and honey producers. Their honey was considered to be of the highest quality in the area; it was derived from the pine trees and the myriad of different flowers that grow at 1,500 meters above sea level.

My paternal grandmother lived with us. She had survived two World Wars raising three children on her own and had once been a cook for the royal family of Habsburg. Her husband died in the First World War and two of her children had been killed in the Second World War; my father was her last remaining immediate family member. While my parents were out all-day farming and collecting honey, my grandmother would take care of us, cooking and caring for us.

During the summer months, we collected many different medicinal herbs, which we dried under the rafters of our large wooden roof. My mother had a profound and extensive knowledge of medicinal herbs and would process them into many different ointments, oils, creams, syrups and soaps. Her natural products were in great demand throughout Tyrol. She was also a trained midwife and was occasionally called to assist in a birth high up in the mountainous regions, where it would be difficult to get hold of a doctor at short notice.

I don't remember a doctor ever coming to our house. Both my mother and grandmother were highly skilled in the use of herbal medicine, and I'm grateful that they passed on much of their knowledge to me; I've put many of their practices to good use on my own family. My mother was a passionate healer and we had all heard the story of how she cured my father's severe rheumatism.

My father returned from the Second World War, after having spent time as a prisoner of war in the Soviet Union, suffering from rheumatism. As the years wore on, it steadily worsened and by the time he was only 36, he could only walk with the assistance of two sticks. Finally, my mother vowed to cure him. She gently massaged his back and legs with her homemade ointments before making him sit in front of an infrared lamp. She continued this treatment for months, and gradually my father's health improved to the point where he only needed one stick to walk with. My mother continued her treatment and eventually my father was able to walk unassisted and was completely free of pain. He always credited his recovery to the love and care of my mother, "my beloved wife" as he used to call her. It was actually my mother's unconditional love that eventually healed him.

They were truly devoted to each other until the very last moments of their lives.

While the summer months were truly idyllic in our region, the long, harsh winters were always a struggle. Our house was often completely covered in snow for weeks on end. Sometimes the snow came right up to the first floor so we could only get in and out of the house via the veranda! My siblings and I spent the long and dark winter days playing with our self-made wooden toys, or we watched our grandmother cook and bake.

My grandmother made the most delicious meals I have ever tasted and she could bake wonderful cakes out of the simplest ingredients. I vividly remember her cake-making ritual. She would hold a large wooden bowl between her knees, into which she would put flour, sugar and some homemade butter. She would start mixing all the ingredients together, and as she stirred, she would literally talk to the cake.

"Oh, are you ready for an egg now?" she would ask it. "And how about a pinch of salt now…, and would you like some milk? How about some nuts?" She would get to the end and suddenly remembered that she had some chocolate in the cupboard, so she had thrown that in at the last minute. She would simply add whatever came to her mind. There was no recipe and no two cakes ever looked or tasted the same. With a big smile on her face, she would then say; "Now, children, today we have a special cake…" with such pride. All my grandmother's cakes were baked—with love and patience—in an old handmade Tyrolean ceramic wood-fired oven. In my whole life, I have honestly never tasted cakes as good as my grandmother's.

I was tremendously excited when the time came for me to start school; I was seven years old—the typical age when Austrian children start school. My brother had been going to school for two whole years before I started, and I couldn't wait for the day when I would be able to go with him. He personally walked me into my classroom on my first day of primary school.

During the winter months, our walk to and from school was rather challenging. We often found ourselves walking through snow that came up to our knees, and with our heavy schoolbags on our shoulders making us sink through the thick snow. Going downhill wasn't so bad, we could put our skis on and travel the three kilometers without too much trouble, but there were no lifts in those days so going back up the hill was a real battle. Some days it was dark before we reached our house because those three kilometers had taken us more than two hours to travel, so our parents would come outside and shine a huge storm torch in our direction, guiding us into the house, like airplanes being brought in to park!

Although I had entered my first school year with huge enthusiasm, it actually turned out to be a bit of a disappointment. No one had noticed, or if they had, they hadn't pointed out to me, that I was completely left-handed. Not only that, but when I started to write, I wrote my letters back-to-front so that the words could only be identified by holding a mirror up to them and reading their reflection.

I was in a class of around 30 pupils and our teacher was an elderly lady with a closed heart. She had probably been teaching for more than 40 years. She was a heavy-handed and demanding teacher who used a cane to strike pupils who did not follow her exact instructions. I did not like her at all. She hardly paid me any attention during my first few months in school except to scrawl across all my homework; "Failed, do it again!" This caused me great distress because I couldn't understand what was wrong; she never explained my mistakes to me. I ended up being so traumatised by the experience of being scolded in class that I temporarily went completely deaf. My mother took me to a doctor who said there was no physical reason for my hearing loss, so it must have been a psychosomatic response.

In those days, children were forbidden from using their left hand to write with. We were forced to use our right hand, which was extremely difficult for me. One day, the teacher stood behind me while we were copying some words down from the blackboard, as per her instructions. After the class, she called me up to her desk and told me I had to bring my parents to see her, because my work was substandard. I was distraught and ashamed. As soon as I was alone I started crying. I cried all the way home, confessing to my brother what had happened. I was worried about my parents' reaction, but my mother could not have been more supportive. She said; "Don't worry, my dear child, you are a highly intelligent girl and your talents will make you famous one day." When I had been made to feel so stupid by my teacher, these words were a great comfort to me. My mother's words became indelibly etched on my heart and whenever I have failed at something in life, they have lifted me up, and given me hope and strength to carry on. I know I can never give up, no matter how many times I fail, because I'm always reminded of my mother's faith in me; indeed, her own tenacity inspired me.

Complying with my teacher's request, my mother accompanied me to school the next day. We went to see my teacher, who told my mother that my work was below standard and that I was not fit to be in her class because my writing was so bad. The teacher explained that she could not give me the required extra attention I needed as she had 30 other pupils to teach. She suggested that my mother should send me to a different school, a school for handicapped children. My world fell apart when I heard this. I was distraught. What made me so different from the other children? I was heartbroken at the idea of not seeing my friends anymore. My mother felt my pain and begged the teacher to keep me. She promised to do everything she could to help me improve my writing.

The teacher agreed to give me a second chance, and, true to her word, my mother spent every moment she could find sitting beside me, helping me learn how to hold a pencil in my right hand and write legibly. Her love and patience changed my life. Had she given in, had she accepted what the teacher had said, I would have been sent to a handicapped school and my life would have followed a very different path. I am sure I would not have achieved the academic qualifications I ended up with. However,

I did not take the experience lightly. I was severely shaken up and it took me years to regain my self-confidence; I probably still bare some of the scars. However, my mother's determination and devotion saved me, and the memory of how she fought for me encouraged me to stand up for myself, and subsequently for my children, when others want to put us down or give up on us. Thankfully, times have changed now and dyslexic or left-handed children are no longer considered as being "disabled."

I remember working tirelessly with my mother to improve my writing. Obviously, after she had fought so hard for me, I didn't want to let her down. Finally, by Easter the following year, thanks to my mother's patience and my diligence, I caught up with my classmates and had mastered an acceptable standard of writing, right-handed. I never really liked my "new" writing style, and for many years I couldn't identify myself with my hand writing, somehow it felt forced, like it wasn't a part of me, but I was aware that I had to conform. Only when I mastered this writing style that was acceptable to my teacher did my hearing gradually come back.

Paris. How did I end up in Paris?

When I was about four years old, I had a vision. I saw myself as a famous singer. I wasn't sure if I was going to be an opera singer or a folk singer, I just knew I was going to be a successful singer, so I started singing and yodeling to my heart's content. Nothing made me feel as good as how I felt when I was singing my heart out. Finally, one day, when I was still relatively young, I confessed my ambition to my father. I was excited about telling him my big news, and I was convinced that he would be proud of me.

I said; "Daddy, guess what? When I grow up I want to be a singer!"

His reaction was not what I expected.

"A singer?" he echoed. "No, my girl, you can't be a singer, a singer doesn't earn money. You need to earn money."

Money? What did I know or care about money?

What I did know was that my father shattered my dreams that day. I didn't challenge him; I accepted what he said. In that moment, the future I had imagined slipped through my fingers and I was completely deflated.

A few years later, when I was around 13 years old, I had another dream. This time I saw myself learning four languages and traveling the world. This was a particularly strong vision and one that stayed with me for many years. I didn't share this new dream with my father, but obviously, what he had said the first time had made a big impression on me because I put all my efforts into earning money. I did any odd job I could find on weekends and during my summer holidays, and I saved every penny I earned. I saved and saved; my sights were set on saving enough money to be able to support myself through continuing my education at University.

In my final year of high school, I passed my entry exams and was awarded a place at a University in Paris. What an achievement for the little girl who had been dismissed by that stern teacher! I could hardly believe it. When I told my father that I was going to Paris to study for a degree in Translation, Interpretation and Psychology, he didn't reply. Perhaps he would have preferred to hear that I was getting a job and earning money instead of continuing my studies, but he must have realised that I was too old, by then, for him to be able to change my mind. All he asked me was if I can afford to go, and whether I have the money to support myself through my studies in Paris. I explained that I had enough money to get me there and start my life because I had been saving every penny I had earned from my summer and weekend jobs. I planned to do whatever part-time work I could get once I arrived in Paris, anything that would fit around my studies. I rarely asked my parents for money to support me through University. I vowed to earn my own money and pay my own way. This attitude continued throughout my life; I never wanted to rely on anyone else for my livelihood. The feeling of wanting to be independent has never left me.

I had been offered a place at the Université de la Sorbonne Nouvelle—Paris III. There was a two-year foundation course to complete before I went on to study for the main degree. During the first year, we would be studying the French language, and during the second year we would learn all about the French literature, culture and history. It was fascinating learning about the French history in the 19th Century, through the novelists of the time, such as Émile Zola, Honoré de Balzac, Guy de Maupassant, Gustave Flaubert and many others. These courses were mandatory for all the students and led us to qualify for our diplôme supérieur. After this foundation course, those who wanted could continue their studies to qualify with a diploma to teach French as a foreign language, or could go on to study for a degree, which was my plan.

I vividly remember arriving in Paris; it was a Tuesday in the first week of September 1971. My suitcases had been packed for weeks and I couldn't wait for my new life to start. I had been pouring over books and newspapers about Paris, soaking up all the information I could find about this wonderful and exciting cosmopolitan city that was a world away from everything I was used to in my rural town in Austria.

On the Monday night, my parents, sister and grandmother took me to the station where I boarded the night train to Paris. They all hugged me tightly, my parents bombarding me with advices and warnings about taking care of myself, obviously anxious about sending their innocent eldest daughter off to another country. I was only 19 years old at the time.

I was too excited to sleep on the train that night, and I sat in my seat watching other passengers, wondering what was taking them to the famous French capital. I must have dozed off eventually because I awoke suddenly, hearing the guard announcing that the time was 6:45 a.m. and we would be arriving in Paris in 15 minutes. I stared out of the window as the train slowly pulled into the biggest, most beautiful train station I had ever seen in my life; we had arrived at *Gare de l'Est*.

A few minutes later, I was standing on the platform with my two big suitcases. I picked them up and carried them out to the street where, following my parents' instructions, I took a taxi straight to the student hostel on the Boulevard du Montparnasse in the *14th arrondissement*, which I had reserved for my first week in the city while I looked for a permanent place. The taxi driver was very kind and spoke to me in a mix of German and English to make me feel welcome. By contrast, the elderly Parisian woman who greeted me at the hostel spoke only French and abruptly showed me to my room; the smallest room I had ever seen in my life. I had honestly seen bigger cupboards. It was like a little cage, but at least it had a window. I also knew I would only be spending a few hours sleeping there as I would be out and about during the day, and it was only for a week. Plus, the excitement of my new adventure overcame any major feelings of disappointment.

Later that day, I went to find my new school, which was located in the *6th arrondissement*. Having arrived at my school, I completed all the formalities associated with the registration for my course and spent quite some time marveling at the architecture and history that surrounded me in the old building, in particular the spectacular staircase monopolizing the grand entrance hall. Along the main corridor, I found a big noticeboard full of school announcements and advertisements for accommodation. I noticed that some of them offered free accommodation and a daily meal in exchange for four hours of work per day. This sounded like an excellent idea and I noted the name and phone number of one couple whose address was close to my University.

When I called the number from the advertisement, the man who answered sounded polite and friendly, but I struggled to understand him because my French was still very basic. However, we finally managed to understand each other and he invited me to come and look at the accommodation. He suggested I should take a taxi and he spontaneously offered to pay for it, which was very kind, but I explained to him, in my broken French, that I would prefer to walk. I told him that I had a good map and wanted to learn my way around the streets. After all, I was confident that I would not get lost!

Later that afternoon, I arrived at the address, a big apartment building on *La Rue du Dragon* in the famous *Saint German-des-Prés* area. I knew I was at the right address because there was a big sign fixed to the wall with the name of the man I had spoken to earlier on it. He was an ophthalmologist who had a clinic and an apartment in the building. I rang the bell and the concierge, a friendly mature woman, opened the main door. I showed her the name and address of the doctor, and she pointed to a staircase at the end of the corridor.

I walked up to the first floor and rang the doorbell. After a few seconds, a man opened the door and from his voice I assumed that he must be the doctor with whom I had spoken earlier on the phone. He greeted me with a warm and friendly smile, invited me in and introduced me to his wife. They were a middle-aged couple who—I soon discovered—did not have any children. As I sat down in the salon, I immediately felt at home. They offered me a glass of French wine, but I kindly told them that I was not used to drinking wine and asked for some milk instead. They found this amusing and explained me that, in France, only small children drink milk. Still, they kindly gave me the glass of milk I had asked for and the incident served as a good ice-breaker, as we began to talk about the French life and Parisian traditions, everything sounding so different from all that I was used from my upbringing in an Austrian village. The conversation led to what would be expected of me in return for the accommodation and meals. I would have to do some light cleaning and help out in the clinic, mostly with the administration of the doctor's patients. The doctor and his wife seemed very flexible and said I could fit the four hours of work in around my studies.

Eventually, they suggested that we go and take a look at the accommodation. The room was what is known as a *chamber de bonne*, an attic bedroom that would have once been used for a member of the household's domestic staff. There were a few of these rooms along the corridor at the top of the building, and there was a shared shower and a toilet one floor below. Even though the room was small, it seemed like a luxury accommodation compared to the cage I had found myself in at the hostel that morning.

By the time I had seen the room and agreed on all the terms, as well as made arrangements for me to move in the next day, it was late at night, and the doctor insisted on paying for a taxi to take me back to the hostel. This time I accepted his offer and thanked him for his kind gesture.

As soon as I entered the taxi, I felt a huge sense of relief that I had found a good and safe family to live with so quickly.

Something told me that life was going to take care of me well during my time in Paris.

I quickly grew to love my new room; there was one large window in it and as the room was on the sixth floor it was filled with light during the day because there were still no big skyscrapers in the center of Paris (as there are in so many other capital cities) to obscure the view. What I wasn't aware of at that moment and I only realised after some time living in there was that it did make the room very hot in the summer, with all that sunlight streaming in. I had a single bed and a small table with two chairs. I used one chair to sit on to study and eat, and the other chair served me well as a nightstand. There was also a small wardrobe and an old refrigerator; after all there was space for little else. I cooked on a tiny camping stove that sat on a shelf above the refrigerator; it was primitive, but I never complained or thought of myself as anything other than being incredibly fortunate for having the opportunity to live and study in Paris. To me, a girl used to the simple Austrian-way of life, I was incredibly fortunate and felt like being the luckiest person in the world, living in such a glamorous and cosmopolitan city like Paris.

My hosts and I quickly formed a close bond. Because they had no children of their own, I was like a daughter to them. The doctor's wife worked for the government, so they were both busy people, but they were very accommodating. As long as I completed my tasks at some point during the day, they were perfectly happy. In the doctor's clinic, I would help him with his patient files, making appointments and doing other small jobs, such as cleaning the lenses he had used after each appointment. Sometimes I would cook the evening meal, according to the wife's instructions. They also helped me with my studies. In the evenings, we often sat together and discussed my University assignments. This was an enormous help to me, especially in the first two years while I was working hard to improve my French. In exchange, I taught them some German and English; it was a win-win situation. However, Paris was still expensive and so I also did some typing work in the evenings, to earn a little extra money. I had an old Brother typewriter and I would type up work for post-graduate students. I spent hours and hours typing during those years in Paris.

There are many famous Parisian places located in the *6th arrondissement*, such as the iconic *Saint Suplice church* and *Le Jardin du Luxembourg*, and part of the Latin Quarter is within that *6th arrondissement*. But the area is perhaps most famous for its cafés, where many famous artists and writers used to meet and collaborate together, the most notable of which are *Café de Flore* and *Les deux Magots*. One can still see old and faded pictures of their famous customers on the walls, such as Picasso, Ernest Hemingway, Albert Camus and many others. Little of the décor has been changed since that period, so it's like taking a step back in time.

During my first few weeks, I walked everywhere in order to help me find my way around. I felt like a stranger, wandering the narrow streets that were full of history and bustling with Parisian life, wondering if I would ever fit in. I spent days with my nose buried in the famous *Plan de Paris par Arrondissement*, walking continuously and sometimes getting lost. I was often approached by men, as I stood on a street corner studying my map with a puzzled look on my face, who would offer to help me and guide me to where I wanted to go. I took heed of the warnings my host had given me about such men, however, I always politely refused their help. The walking never bothered me; I was used to walking long distances in the Austrian mountains and this was how I actually discovered the magic of Paris. Every time I got lost and found myself on an unfamiliar street, I discovered a new treasure; a little church, a café, a fountain or a statue, for example. There is always more to discover in Paris. No matter how long you spend wandering the streets of France's capital city, you can never know every corner.

I was passionate about visiting museums. One of my favorites was *Le Louvre*, where I spent many Sundays walking through the endless rooms, marveling at the art from every age, and watching da Vinci's painting of *Mona Lisa* "follow me" with her famous eyes. I could sit in front of that painting for hours. I loved the "Winged Victory of Samothrace," which was estimated to have been created around 200 BC by an unknown Greek artist. I was transfixed by that headless marble statue; it inspired me with its message of freedom and liberty. I was also deeply inspired by Rodin's "Thinker" whenever I visited the *Musée Rodin*, not only because it radiated power and wisdom, but also because every muscle in the body was represented so naturally; it's quite beautiful to behold. Another favorite museum of mine was the *Musée de l'Orangerie*, in the *Jardin des Tuileries*. There was a whole section of the museum dedicated to the works of Claude Monet, where his huge paintings were displayed in the large whitewashed rooms. The atmosphere in there was so peaceful and calming.

I have always found great comfort in immersing myself in art, imagining how the artists must have felt while creating their work. The museums in Paris are so welcoming and were such great places to spend my days off, by myself, in the weeks before I made some good friends at my University.

Eventually, the romance in the Parisian air took hold of me and I fell in love with a handsome, elegant boy from Madagascar. We were both incredibly shy and the extent of our physical intimacy was to hold hands as we walked around the *Jardin des Tuileries*. At that time and for our age, this was exciting enough! We had many long conversations about all the things we dreamed of doing with our lives. We often went to the cinema together and sometimes to a concert on a weekend. Sadly, the romance came to an end at the end of my second year in Paris because he returned back to Madagascar. He urged me to visit him there, but I knew it would be years before I would have the money to make such a big trip. So, we agreed to keep in touch as friends and not to "wait" for each other. We actually kept a long-distance friendship going for over ten years until he got married and started a family, after which many friendships tend to get lost in the pressures of a busy family life.

My other great friend during these years was a sweet Canadian girl called Caroline, from Toronto, who had come to Paris to study French. We were in the same academic year at University. Caroline was a real natural beauty; she was tall with long brown hair that always looked so healthy and shiny. She had a bubbly, sunny character and was always full of ideas. We did so much together! We explored new places, sometimes by going on a cycling tour; we once cycled 40 kilometers around Paris, which we later called this "*Le tour de Paris.*" Also, I will never forget the great picnics we had, sitting under a tree in the *Bois de Boulogne.* I am sure Paris is the picnic capital of the world; it's so easy to pick up some bread and cheese, and to sit somewhere and eat "al fresco." I couldn't even begin to count the number of little events we attended together, there was always some exhibition or play or concert to go to, plus we went together on excursions to other areas of France. One of my favorite memories was visiting the famous island *Le Mont Saint Michel* in Normandy, which is filled with a rich history. We were excited to see for ourselves this place we had heard so much about, and witness how it's so close to the mainland that, when there is a low tide, you can walk to it on foot. We were interested to see how many pilgrims had traveled to visit the abbey there. The whole area is steeped in such rich and interesting history that it's easy to understand why it has been classified as a UNESCO World Heritage Site.

I also formed a close friendship with a Greek girl called Ianthe. She was from Athens and had also come to study French in Paris because she wanted to work as a French teacher in Greece. She loved to sing and dance, especially the traditional Greek dances, and took me to various Greek Taverns in Paris, where I learned to dance the famous Greek *Sirtaki* dance.

Most of these adventures took place during weekends. I was very busy working and studying during the rest of the week, but I always had the weekends off to enjoy Paris and partake in many new experiences with my friends.

My new life in Paris was incredibly exciting, and I was so busy every day that I found it hard to remember to contact my parents regularly and let them know how I was getting on. By that time, my parents had moved to a new area and had no phone in their house. The only place they could make and receive phone calls was in the village post office, so our communication was limited to letter writing once a month.

However, doesn't time fly when you're having fun?

One day, I had the shock of my life. As I was working in the doctor's surgery room one afternoon, there was a sudden knock on the door. I opened the door and saw two policemen standing there. They said that they were looking for a certain *mademoiselle* from Austria. I told them that I was she. They asked me to contact my parents urgently in Austria. I was extremely worried that something terrible had happened so I made a call that very afternoon to the company where my father worked. He nearly had a heart attack when he heard my voice, however, once he got over the relief of hearing from me I could tell that he was rather angry. He asked me how I could possibly let three months go by without sending any word to him and my mother, to let them know how I was. I was truly shocked; I had no idea that three months had passed by, but they had, and they had been worried sick about me. In desperation, my mother had eventually contacted *Interpol* to ask them to search for me in Paris! I felt so ashamed.

I was so young and enthralled with my new life, that was full of adventures and challenges, that I had become completely wrapped up in my own world; it wasn't until many, many years later, when I became a mother myself, that I fully understood what my mother must have gone through at that time and I felt terribly guilty about it in retrospect. All I could do at the time was to write a letter to my parents, apologizing deeply for causing them so much anguish and begging for forgiveness. I couldn't believe that I had let so much time go by; I felt awful when I pictured my mother waiting anxiously for a letter from her daughter in Paris, starting to wonder whether she was alive or dead.

Towards the end of 1974, and after having lived for four years in France, I was in the second year of studying Translation, Interpretation and Psychology, when money really got tight. I wrote and told my parents that I would not be able to come home for Christmas that year, as I had done every year previously. This, however, was not acceptable to my parents and they immediately sent me the money for a train ticket to Austria. Four months later, I came to understand why they had generously given me the money to make that trip back home for Christmas.

Christmas was always a wonderful and joyful time with my family in Austria. That year, I remember it being a particularly happy year. My brother and sister were both living in Germany by then. My brother was married and had two small children and my sister was in her first year of nursing college, but they had both come back to Austria for Christmas—my brother arriving with his whole family. My siblings had to leave to get back to Germany a few days after Christmas, but I didn't have to be back in Paris until the first week of January, when my course started again. So, I was left to enjoy my last few days of my holidays with my parents and grandmother, before I returned to Paris.

On the day I was due to leave, my father accompanied me to the train station and when the time came for us to say goodbye, I was shocked to see that he had big tears in his eyes. And, out of the blue he said; "I feel like I won't see you again."

Then he kissed me and left abruptly. I felt so confused as I watched him walk away. What did he mean? Was he worried something bad would happen to me in Paris? The question occupied my mind during the whole train ride back to Paris and I promised to myself to write them more often. Once I got back to Paris, however, I got swept up into my old busy life routine, and with all the pressures of studying for my end of the year exams, I only managed to write them once a month as usual.

I spent April studying whenever and wherever I could, preparing for my big end-of-year exams that were scheduled to take place sometime towards the end of May. I hardly noticed the days whizzing by. That is, until the 8th of May, the day before my 23rd

birthday, when time seemed to have reached to an abrupt end, and my life changed forever.

When I arrived home from University that day, the doctor gave me an urgent telegram that had just arrived. I had the most terrible sinking feeling in my heart as he handed it to me. I could feel the color draining from my face and I felt as if I was going to faint. I excused myself, telling the doctor I needed to lie down. I went to my room clutching this telegram in my hand. I didn't want to read it; I was terrified. I had a sixth sense that this telegram was going to be some awful news. I sat down on the edge of my bed and finally found the courage to open the telegram. It simply said; "Father died, funeral 12th of May. Brother, John." I couldn't stop staring at these words. I felt as if my heart had stopped beating and that the time was standing still. I wanted to wind back the clock and undo this from happening. The whole room became filled with sadness as a terrible weight sat on my shoulders, and I felt as though my whole body was filled with blackness. At first, I couldn't feel or show any emotions. Also, I couldn't imagine drinking, eating or sleeping. I didn't even feel as if I was alive and being in a human body; I felt as if I was one of Rodin's marble statues, headless.

I didn't know what to do; I must have sat, motionless, on the edge of my bed for many hours. I knew there was no point in trying to call my brother, as he must have already left his house in Germany to make the six-hour drive to our village in Austria. Memories of my childhood flooded my mind; I pictured my father and all the happy times we had together; it was like watching a movie of my life with him in it. But still, I felt emotionally paralysed.

Finally, I looked up through my window and realised that dawn was breaking; it was a new day, it was the 9th of May 1975, my 23rd birthday, and suddenly, I felt an intense pain. I wished, with all my heart, that this day had not arrived; it felt wrong that the sun was about to shine, as if it should always be night, because the light that had been the life of my beloved father had been extinguished.

I rushed out of my room without even thinking of changing my clothes, walked downstairs and left the building. I still hadn't shed a tear. I walked down to the river Seine, which was only a short walk from where I lived, and began to walk along the riverbank. The world hasn't woken up yet; everything was so still and quiet in the emerging light of dawn. The Seine has always had a kind of magical effect on me; I find it so tranquil, looking into the river, separating myself from everything in my life for a few moments. That morning it gave me a particular comfort. I focused on the water, and walked beneath the trees, thinking only of the nature, trying to empty my head of any other thoughts.

By the time I returned home, the shops had all opened up for the day and people were going about their regular morning business. I must have been walking for hours. I was desperate to speak to my brother, but there was no way of getting hold of him as there was still no telephone in my parents' house. My greatest concern was my mother's health. How was she coping? What was she feeling? I could hardly bare to think of the pain she must have been experiencing. In that moment, all I wanted to do was tell her that I love her. I wanted to wrap my arms around her and hold her, and reassure her that I was there for her.

I suddenly realised that I had to get on a train immediately. I went to speak to the doctor and told him what had happened. I told him that I had to get home as soon as possible, but I was worried about my exams, that were only a few days away. I poured out my heart to him and he listened, patiently. Then he simply reassured me that he would take care of everything else. The doctor was so supportive. He actually bought my train ticket himself, sent a telegram to my mother to inform her when the train would arrive, and then he spoke to my tutor and managed to arrange for my exams to be postponed until September. After that, I called my Canadian friend Caroline, who cried with me when she heard the news.

I remember I arrived at the train station long before the departure time of my train. I sat on a bench, waiting. I still felt numb; my heart was already in Austria with my family, with my Mum.

Only my physical body was still here, sitting on that hard, cold bench in *Gare de l'Est*, while watching people come and go; who they all looked considerably happier than me.

That ten-hour train journey felt like the longest journey I had ever taken in my life. I couldn't eat or sleep. I even, couldn't read or speak a word. I wouldn't have known what to say to anyone; there were no words to describe what I was feeling. I could think of nothing but getting back home, to be with my Mum. All I wanted was to see my mother, the person who had saved my life from being put in a mentally handicapped school. I couldn't wait to see her eyes, to hug her and to tell her, how much I love her. This is all I have now, a voice kept telling me. The moment the train arrived in Salzburg and I saw her, I flung myself into her arms and held her for what felt like hours on end. I had never before felt such pain in my chest. Seeing my mother with such intense sadness in her eyes from her broken heart, having lost her beloved husband, her one and only love, was unbearable. We couldn't stop crying. My brother and sister were there too, with red eyes from crying so much. Finally, we left the station and made our way home. I couldn't even imagine our house without my father in it and I knew another tragic sight awaited me at home; the vision of my grandmother, my wonderful grandmother, who I imagined, must have been in such tremendous pain. I pictured her crying her eyes out at having lost her last remaining child. However, when I saw her, she actually looked quite composed! She was clearly sad, but there was so much strength in her eyes. She simply looked at me and said; "When this kind of tragedy strikes in life, my child, if it doesn't kill you, it only makes you stronger."

Much later that evening, I sat with my mother and asked her to explain what had happened, to tell me how my father had died. She explained that he had been having some bad pains in his stomach for several months. In the end, it got worse and the pain occurred so regularly that they got him an appointment at the hospital for an endoscopy. During the procedure, my father had suddenly stopped breathing and his heart stopped. By the time they realised what had happened, it was too late. Their efforts to resuscitate him failed; he was gone.

Meanwhile, my mother had been sitting outside the operation room waiting for news of her husband's routine procedure. The next thing she knew, a nurse was sitting next to her, telling her that her husband had died from heart failure. I listened as my mother told me this story in precise detail, wishing I could relieve her from her pain. Her world had been shattered, her heart had been ripped apart, and I could do nothing to stop her from been hurt. I had never felt so awful and useless in all my life.

The next day was the funeral. My brother and sister had arrived from Germany two days before me, so they had already made the necessary arrangements. The funeral was a traditional village one, with friends, relatives and colleagues attending, along with hundreds of villagers. There were many tears, and the local music band played some traditional songs as we made our procession to the church. I will never forget watching my 84-year-old grandmother standing by my father's coffin saying her last goodbye to him. At the age of 24, she lost her husband in the First World War. Then, at the age of 54, she also lost two of her sons in the Second World War, and now, she had to say goodbye to her last child, my father, who just turned 63 years of age. I have never met someone so brave. I often think of that moment; watching her in the church, when I need strength. She remains, to this day, my all-time heroine and role model.

In the days after my father's funeral, we had many visitors coming to our family home; there was a constant stream of people paying their respects. Our only peace came at night, when we sat together in silence and held hands, trying to deal with the enormous weight and agony of our grief. This was when we did our crying, when we let our emotions surface. Every night, I slept in my mother's bed so she wouldn't feel being alone. Every night, she prayed out loud before closing her eyes; "Please God, take me home to be with my beloved husband." Although this bothered me, hearing my mother saying these words, I knew I had to let her do whatever she needed to do.

My brother and sister left for Germany a few days after the funeral, but I was able to stay for two weeks before I had to return back to Paris. During that time, I put all my focus on making my mother's life as easy as possible. My grandmother did all the cooking and I spent every waking moment at my mother's side. Together we did simple things, like some digging in the garden or making flower arrangements to take to my father's grave. We did whatever my mother felt like doing; this was her time to do as she pleased. I often think back to this special time with my mother and feel happy to think of how much love and support I was able to give her in her time of great grief.

Finally, it was time for me to leave for Paris. Before my brother and sister had left, we had arranged all the formalities to do with our father's death and had dealt with all the inheritance matters, so that our mother wouldn't be confronted with any paperwork. We had also agreed that I would come and spend a month with our mother as soon as my exams were over in September. My brother and sister agreed that they would each come and spend a month with her during the summer holidays, between July and August. We didn't want her to spend too much time alone, without at least one of us there to support and comfort her.

When we arrived at the train station, my mother looked me straight in the eyes, hugged me and told me how much she loved me. Then she said; "You need to carry on with your life; I belong to my husband."

Her words scared me, even though they didn't really make sense to me at that time. I quickly told her how much we all loved her and reminded her that she would get so much joy from watching her grandchildren grow up! She did not reply. I left for Paris feeling as uneasy as I had felt when my father had left me at the station four months earlier.

I arrived back in Paris sometime during the last week of May and started to reconnect with my life there. I found it very hard to get back to my usual Parisian life and I was glad that the doctor and his wife were so helpful and compassionate. They spent many evenings talking with me about what had happened. They were so kind, and I felt completely supported and loved, which eased my grieving process a little. I threw myself back into my studies and got absorbed in a summer cultural program. My friends were also extremely supportive, and I constantly felt as if I was being wrapped up in a warm blanket of friendship.

I was thankful that I had plenty of time to prepare for my exams in September. August, in particular, is always a very quiet time in Paris since the locals tend to leave, *"en masse,"* for their holiday homes in the countryside or the famous resorts along the south and west coasts. I felt secure and strong as I kept myself busy with my Parisian life, but I just couldn't stop thinking of my mother and grandmother, and wonder how they were coping. I imagined how sad they would be, day in, day out, without my father's presence. My dear mother was in my mind constantly. No matter what I was doing, no matter what I was talking about and feeling on the surface, deep down I never stopped thinking about my mother. For several weeks after I arrived back in Paris, I was still waking up in the middle of the night thinking about her and worrying about her.

The 5th of June was my father's birthday, so I thought it would be the perfect time to write my mother a beautiful letter, to remind her that I was constantly thinking of her, that I love her, and to distract her from her grief, by telling her about some of the exciting things I was getting up to in Paris. I was aware that my letter would probably not arrive for a few days after I sent it because the postal service at that time was slow, but I hoped my mother would send me a reply as soon as she received it. However, ten days later, I still hadn't heard from her and I was beginning to feel a little uneasy. I had spent many evenings walking through the streets of Paris alone, trying to rid my head of the disturbing thoughts that kept coming up, that reminded me of the strange way in which my mother had said goodbye to me. I prayed that she was coping somehow, that she was not in too much pain.

On the 16th of June, I arrived home very late, after one of my long walks; it was after 10 p.m. I was tired and not particularly hungry, so I decided to go straight to bed without eating my dinner. This wasn't an unusual occurrence; I often skipped meals during those weeks following my father's death. I must have lost more than 6 kilograms in just over a month.

I went straight into my bed and read a book for a while, before turning out my light shortly after midnight. I must have fallen into a deep sleep because it felt like a split of a second later that I woke up abruptly, thinking that I had heard someone calling my name. I tried to open my eyes, looked at my alarm clock standing on the chair next to my bed, and saw that it was 5 a.m., but there was only silence and darkness around me, so I turned over and tried to get back to sleep. This time I didn't go back to sleep so quickly. Some time passed, as I lay in bed, wide awake, trying to get back to sleep, before I suddenly heard the creaking of the wooden staircase that led up to my floor. I held my breath as I concentrated on listening carefully. I could hear footsteps approaching my door. Then they stopped. Next, it sounded as if someone was trying to push something under my door. I immediately sat up and looked at the door. I recognised there was something on the floor that looked like a letter. The footsteps were now retreating from my room, and I soon heard them going back down the creaking staircase. Finally, I heard the entrance door of the building close with a loud bang. The moment I looked at this letter behind my door, I felt a strong sharp pain in my entire body and my heart started palpitating in my throat; again, I knew this was something terrible, I felt it in my bones. For a moment, I convinced myself and I strongly hoped that this was my mother's reply to my earlier letter to her.

I got out of my bed and picked up what I now recognised as a telegram. I sat on my bed holding it, with my eyes burning. No, please, I thought, not again. Please, it cannot be. Slowly, I pulled myself together and opened the telegram. There were the words I dreaded most; "Mother died. Please come home immediately. Brother, John." My heart broke apart and my world collapsed forever.

Passing of my parents. I was sure; I was dead. I stared at the piece of paper in my hands without any thoughts coming into my head. I was frozen in time. I could see the words, but it was as if they were written in a different language, one I couldn't understand. I felt completely empty, there were no emotions inside me, no thoughts, nothing. Surely, I had died too. This had to be death, this feeling of nothingness. I couldn't even feel my hands; I had to be dead. I hoped I was dead.

As if I was a robot, re-running a program that I had completed six weeks earlier. Unable to move, I waited until dawn broke and the light started to come through my window, before I rose from my bed, holding the paper still tightly in one hand. I left the house. I kept walking, heading towards the river like a zombie and started that familiar journey along the riverbank. I was completely numb, emotionless. I had shed so many tears in the past few weeks, and as much as I tried, there were none left to shear. I simply walked forwards, trying to leave life behind me, as if I could walk away from my current reality and enter into a world where my mother and father still live happily together.

I focused on the river, on the pairs of ducks swimming along happily, on the empty tourist boats waiting for a busy day of river tours, on the empty bottles and remnants of picnics left by the river wall; it's amazing how much detail you absorb when your mind is completely empty of all thoughts and emotions. My current world contained only these basic things I could see around me.

As I approached *Pont Neuf*, I noticed a number of *clochards* (vagrants) sleeping rough under the bridge. They were covered with dirty old blankets and scattered around them were empty bottles that had contained all the alcohol that these men had consumed until they fell unconscious, enabling them to sleep through such terrible conditions. The familiar smell of urine mixed with cheap wine and stale beer reached me, and, as if the smell awakened my stunned brain, thoughts began creeping into my mind. What was I doing? Why was I here? Why wasn't I at home packing to leave for Austria? Why wasn't I trying to contact my brother and sister to tell them I was on my way? Why wasn't I asking the doctor to help me? Why wasn't I calling my friends to tell them of this tragedy? I was doing none of these things. Why? Instead, I was trying to escape my existence by walking along the *Quai de Conti,* staring at ducks and empty boats and the unconscious vagrants. Strange isn't it? But at this moment, I felt totally connected to these poor souls who were living a rough life. I wondered what had put them in this position. Perhaps they had lost their loved ones and were waiting to die. With the look at these men, I asked myself, what's the point of living if you lose the people you love the most? What is the meaning of life without the people who had always been at the center of your world and whose love had always filled the very core of your being? Is it really worth staying alive to be so alone? How could the future possibly hold any happiness if my beloved parents were not there to share it with me? All these questions turned round and round in my mind with no answers.

Eventually, I arrived at *Boulevard Saint Michel* in the Latin Quarter and saw that the huge bookstore *Gibert Jeune* was just opening its doors. Without a second thought and as I was still in a total daze, I found myself walking towards it and going inside. I started wandering aimlessly amongst these endless long and heavy packed bookshelves, glancing at titles. Between the rows of these bookshelves, there were long tables with books displayed on them. As I cast my eyes over the cover photos of random books on the table displays, one particular cover caught my attention. I looked closer and saw a middle-aged man wrapped in a blanket, like a Buddhist monk, standing upright, staring at a heap of smoldering ashes, holding a half-burned sandal in his hand. It made me become curious, so I picked up the book and read what said on the back of the cover. The man on the cover portrayed exactly how I felt. All of a sudden, I felt as though I had been drawn into the bookstore with the sole purpose of finding this book. The title of the book was *"Au nom de tous les miens"* (For Those I Loved) and the author's name said Martin Grey; I knew how well I could identify myself with his story and I felt as though I had to read it straight away. In my pocket I had a few coins that could have bought me a coffee and a croissant, but with the given circumstances I had no stomach for any food or drink, all I wanted was to get this book, and so, I spent every last penny I had on me to get it.

With the book in my hands, I walked back down to the river, I sat down on a bench nearby and opened the book. As I started to read, the sun came out and I perceived the general buzz of life around me. The *Boulevard Saint Michel* was coming alive with traffic and pedestrians. For a moment, I forgot everything, in fact I actually felt some strange happiness as I buried myself in the book and cut off the world around me. I quickly became completely absorbed in the words under my nose.

The book's story was about the life journey of a Polish man. He explained how, after having survived the Holocaust, he escaped to America where he had started a family. They had subsequently come to live in France and moved into a beautiful wooden house, surrounded by a vast forest. One day, as he returned from his business trip, he found that his entire house was completely burned down, killing his wife and their four young children. There had been a devastating forest fire and the family had been unable to escape from the house on time. A huge pile of ash was all that remained of this man's house and beloved ones. As sad as his story was, however reading about his terrible discovery, about his heart-breaking pain and the way how he tried to cope was somehow comforting me. I didn't feel so alone anymore. This was the first of many times throughout my life when the right book has found me exactly at the moment I've needed it the most. I read it hungrily, desperate to allow the details to distract me from my own life. I didn't stop reading until it was midday and I could feel my head starting to burn from the hot sun that was blazing overhead.

I knew it was time to go home.

I decided to go and see my tutor at the University as it was on my way home. Even though we had finished classes for the summer and the school was officially closed, the professors were still working. Still, with the book in my hands I slowly walked into the main entrance hall of the University and found one of the secretaries. I asked if I could speak to Professor Durand, my favorite tutor. I was extremely fond of this rather jolly, elderly man. He had a big heart and would always go out of his way to help us with our studies. I also happened to know that he had lost his wife a few years earlier.

I sat in the waiting area while the secretary went to find the professor. I remained calm and composed while I sat there waiting, but as soon as I saw my tutor's kind face as he came down the stairs and started to approach me, I broke down. Tears emerged from somewhere and flooded down my cheeks. I was unable to speak, I was crying so hard. He took my hand, guided me into his office and sat by my side while I found the strength to speak. Finally, I poured it all out, telling him everything that had happened to me over the past six weeks. I told him about the telegram informing me of my father's death, about the time I spent with my mother in Austria, about the strange way in which she had bid me farewell at the station, and then I showed him the telegram I had received that morning.

I will never forget the kindness and love that this man showed me; it was like having a father beside me. He took my hand, gently, and spoke to me like a father would speak to his daughter. He said that I was a brave young girl; he assured me that I had a great strength inside me, and that this strength would serve me well throughout my life. He told me he was sure I would be very successful in whatever I chose to do because of my inner strength. I was obviously worried about my exams in September, but he told me not to think about any of that now. He said I should go home to Austria and attend to family matters first. He advised me to give myself a few weeks off and then take some time to think things through before I made any decisions regarding my exams. While still holding my hand, he proposed me to contact him when I was ready and said that he would support me with whatever I decided to do.

Listening to his comforting words made me feel so good and I left with some weight lifted off my shoulders. My tutor's words had given me a new strength and comforted me, when I needed it most.

Next, I went to see Caroline. She was preparing to return to Canada for the summer holidays as she had completed her exams in May and her second year of studies in Paris was over. She had been excited about the prospect of spending her final few days with me. She was stunned when I arrived to tell her what had happened, we hugged each other and shed many tears together, for my mother as well as in great sadness at our parting.

Telling the doctor and his wife hit me the hardest of all. They had been like my Parisian parents and cared about me as if I was their own child, so they were naturally devastated for me. They asked me what my plans were, but I couldn't possibly say at that point. The only thing I could think about in that moment was getting back to Austria and seeing my siblings, my brother and sister. I couldn't think beyond that. I packed up the few personal possessions I had into a small suitcase, leaving less important things behind. The next thing I clearly remember was standing in the street, clutching the book I had bought earlier in my hand, waving goodbye to this wonderful couple. We were all crying. I remember the certainty I felt that this house was no longer going to be my home; the sadness of this terrible thought crushed me even further.

I had completely lost memory of how I got to the train station, but suddenly, I was aware that I was at *Gare de l'Est*, sitting in the departure hall, on the exact same bench that I sat six weeks earlier, as I had waited to board the train to go home for my father's funeral. What a twisted irony, I thought, as I prayed out loud, under my breath.

"Please, God," I said. "Please, please be beside me now because I really don't know what will happen to me and my future. All I know is that, I am so scared."

The overwhelming emotion I felt was deep sadness, but I was also terrified about what was going to happen to me. I really felt as though, my life had come to an end. I couldn't see the future; I couldn't begin to imagine what was in store for me. I felt as though, the events of the past six weeks—losing both my parents so suddenly—had changed the course of my life. I was sure; I would never be able to go back to Paris and finish my studies. I felt as though the academic qualifications I had dreamed of achieving since I was a young girl were now out of my grasp. I couldn't see one single thing to feel any happiness or hope about. My mother and father were dead, my life in Paris had come to an abrupt end and my dream was over. What was going to happen with me?

I thought nothing could ever be as bad as the train journey I had taken six weeks earlier, when I was on the way to my father's funeral, but this one was at least five times more miserable; it felt final somehow. With every mile we traveled, there was more distance between me and Paris, and the life I had briefly tasted and loved so dearly. I buried myself in Martin Grey's book. His misery was perversely comforting. His story was so dramatic, it absorbed my full attention, and it helped me to feel that someone had gone through events even worse than those that had turned my life upside down.

My brother and sister were waiting for me at the station when I arrived. We hugged but we had no words, and our tears had all been shed, so there was simply a deadened silence between us.

I soon learned about the last hours of my mother's life. She had been on her bicycle, on her way to visit my father's grave to water the flowers she had planted there, when she suffered a heart attack. She was dead by the time the ambulance arrived. I felt a small amount of relief in the knowledge that she had died so suddenly; we were hopeful that she had not experienced too much pain. It all sounded as though she had literally died of a broken heart; it seems to be quite common for couples who are very close and have lived many, many years together to die within weeks of each other. And my parents were incredibly close. After their youngest child, my sister, had left home to go and study in Germany, my parents had enjoyed what felt like, to them, a second honeymoon period. For the first time in their lives, they didn't have too many responsibilities. They had really struggled when we were young and they had worked so hard to provide us with the right foundations. After we all grew up and left home, they suddenly found that they had plenty of time on their hands to really enjoy each other's company. They had been pursuing all kinds of hobbies and had rekindled their relationship with great passion. We all knew how happy they were; their love for each other was deep and endless. That's why it wasn't too surprising that my mother was, literally, unable to live without her closest friend and soulmate. For her, life had no real meaning without my father around. Our spirits were somewhat lifted to think that, in death, our mother had been reunited with the love of her life. This was what she had prayed for; this was where she wanted to be.

A couple of days later, we buried my mother. The day was a beautiful one, even though our hearts were filled with an almost unbearable pain of sadness. All my parents' friends and distant relatives came, and I am sure the whole village turned out that day. The same musicians played the same piece of music they had played at my father's funeral only a few weeks before; it was all like a *déjà vu*. I can still see myself standing in front of my mother's coffin saying goodbye, telling her how much I love and miss her, wishing her happiness in joining my father, telling them both to watch over us, and crying until I thought my heart would break. I couldn't understand how life could be so cruel. Why? Why take these honest and caring people away from their loving children? I was mystified and broken hearted.

As I watched my mother's coffin being lowered, I felt as though I was watching my personal dream being buried with her. I knew there was no way I could continue with my studies now; I had reached a dead end in that respect.

All that was left of our little family unit now was my brother, my sister, my grandmother and myself. We had to figure out how to move forward. One thing my siblings and I were convinced was that we had to do everything we could to ensure our 84-year-old grandmother lived a comfortable life and was taken good care of. She had contributed so much to our family, and we all felt it was our duty to look after her and make her feel safe.

At that moment, my brother was partway through studying to become a sports car designer. He had a life in Germany with his wife and two young children. My sister was at nursing school and was too young to take on much responsibility or make any major changes to her life, so I knew the majority of the practical responsibility would fall on my shoulders.

When my siblings and I had all left home to follow our individual paths with our various studies in foreign cities, my parents had sold our original family home and bought a smaller house in a village near Salzburg, about 200 kilometers from where we had grown up. The house was in a relatively expensive area and needed some renovation work, so they had taken out a mortgage on it. The area was beautiful, it was surrounded by lakes and was particularly picturesque, but it was also a new development, which was why many residences were still without phone lines.

We knew someone had to keep up the mortgage payments on the house or we would have had to sell it. There was no spare cash available; we even had to sell our father's new car to be able to pay for the funeral expenses of both our parents. In any case, even if we had been able to sell the house, there would have been many government inheritance taxes to be paid and all sorts of other expenses that none of us had the money to cover. In addition, the renovations on the house still hadn't been completed. We wouldn't have been able to sell it for what it was worth without completing the work, and obviously, we had no money for that either. There was no other option; someone had to take over the mortgage and the only person potentially in a position to do so was me.

I made a life-changing decision. I told my brother and sister that I would give up my studies in Paris and get a job in order to keep up the mortgage payments and that I would move into our parents' house and look after our grandmother. In that way, I would slowly take over ownership of the house and I would buy my brother and sister out when I had the money to give them their share. They both accepted, providing that they would only get their respective shares of the house when I was in a financial position to buy them out. They were more than happy to agree to this. In fact, they were relieved. Neither of them wanted to move back to Austria at that point or could afford to take on the responsibility of mortgage payments. So, it was decided and agreed upon, and I resigned myself to what was going to be my new life; a life I never expected or wished for, but a life that I had to accept. Perhaps, this was my destiny?

The next morning, I sat with my grandmother and told her that she could stay in the house and that I was going to move back to Austria to take care of her and keep up the mortgage payments. She cried; it was the first time I had ever seen my grandmother cry. After everything she had endured, after the stoicism she showed over losing her last child, nothing had moved her as much as this news. Only when I saw her cry, did I realise how anxious she must have been, thinking that she might lose her home and be all alone in her final years. Seen her cry and feeling her agony, moved me to tears too.

I was obviously devastated for myself, realising that my dream was over. All I knew was that I had a diploma, but it was not the one I had set my heart on, the one that I had studied so hard for, the one I felt sure I needed to set me off on the right career path in life. However, the only consolation I had was that somewhere in my head, a little voice perhaps will tell me that one day, I would be rewarded for the huge sacrifice I had made, that life would pay me back in kind, for the fact that I had given up my dream to look after our grandmother and to take on the responsibility of our home. At my 23 years of age, I had the courage to take on a huge responsibility that wasn't in line with what I had hoped to do with my life. I had to have faith that taking on such a burden would teach me something and strengthen me for any experience I would encounter later on in life. Suddenly, I remembered my mother's words after having been expelled from school.

As the summer drew to a close, I started looking for a job. I managed to secure a suitable position where I could use some of my language skills, working as a receptionist in a four-star hotel in the world's famous ski-resort *Kitzbühel*. The job was well paid and even though it was a 90-minute drive away, the hours would at least allow me to be with my grandmother in the evenings so she wouldn't get lonely. I resolved to borrow the money to buy a small car that I would easily be able to repay with my wages.

But before I started my job, I was fortunately able to return to Paris to tie up some loose ends. My wonderful grandmother generously gave me the money for the train fare plus a little extra so I could invite some friends out to join me for a goodbye coffee. An 84-year-old woman, who had probably never traveled more than 60 kilometers from her home, gave me money from her pension so that I could make a journey that was so important to me. I believe the gesture was very much driven by her gratitude that I had sacrificed my life in Paris so that I could remain in Austria to work and keep up the mortgage payments on the house. With the expectation of the enormous sadness that I would have to face when I got to Paris, I boarded the night train once more.

That overnight journey to Paris was a particularly melancholic one. I was so used to being filled with excitement on this journey, at the prospect of returning to the life I dearly loved. This time, I knew the enjoyment I would feel about being in Paris would be short-lived, as it would be curtailed by my imminent final departure.

When I arrived, early the next morning, I went straight to see the doctor and his wife to tell them about my new plans. We all cried bitterly; they were as disappointed as I was that my life in Paris had to end so abruptly, but they could see that I had no other choice. They were worried for me, concerned that I was starting out in life with such big debts over my head, having to take care of a large mortgage, but they wished me well. Next, I visited my most respectful and caring tutor for the last time in his office and told him about my plans. He totally understood my position and told me how much he admired my braveness. He finally hugged me, which back then it was rather unusual for a person in this position, and told me that hopefully everything goes well with me and my life ahead.

From the University, I was given a certificate to show the modules I had already passed and was told I could return to my studies at any time. Even though it was early September by this time and my second-year exams were technically still scheduled for then, I had been unable to do any studying, so there was no point in taking them at that time. The summer months had been taken up with all the endless inheritance matters and I was physically drained from grieving. I had buried both my parents in such a short period of time and had made a life-altering decision that put an enormous burden on my head. There was not a single brain cell left in my head that could have focused on my studies.

My wonderful tutor sent me a personal letter that touched me so deeply. I will never forget his supportive words. He expressed his great admiration for me, saying that I was an exceptionally strong young woman, and brave to be taking on such a huge but important burden when many others in my age might have crumbled under the weight of what I had experienced. He said that fate must have picked me for great things. Otherwise I wouldn't have been tested with such a weight of responsibility; that I clearly had a very special task ahead of me, for which I would need all the experience I was gathering during these devastating times. He also said I was too young at that point to understand the enormity of the responsibilities that had been put on my shoulders and what it would all be leading to, but that I would understand one day, and then everything would make more sense.

The very same evening, I arranged to meet all my friends in a small traditional French restaurant. They expressed how sad they were to be losing a classmate they loved. They told me how much joy I had brought to their lives, especially because I had the ability to cheer anyone up with my "sunny and humorous" character. Throughout my life, people approached me by saying that I inspire them with my ability to find happiness even during sad times and without needing much in the way of material possessions. I managed to keep in touch with some of these friends and classmates for many years after I left Paris.

The day before I left to go back to Austria, the doctor and his wife took me out for dinner to a really elegant restaurant on the *Champs Elysees*. They kept telling me how much they hoped I would return to finish my studies and that I would always have a home with them if and whenever I did return. I felt so grateful for their love and support. I told them that I too hoped to come back, but that only time would tell where life would take me.

Finally, far too quickly, it was time for me to spend my very last night in my little room, in the city that had become my new home, where my strength had been tested to its limits, as I faced the most terrible loss of both my parents. Strangely, even though I had gone through this terrible experience in Paris, I only felt love for this city. I knew I would miss it deeply; it was the place where I grew to become an adult and I felt it would always hold a very special place in my heart. As I said goodbye to my friends, the places I loved, the life I held so dearly, and the dream I had only just glimpsed, I had to believe that something good lay ahead for me, as my tutor had suggested. Having made such a huge sacrifice, how could it not?

This was how I began my new life in Austria, working during day-time in the hotel and keeping my grandmother company in the evenings. We sat together during the long, dark winter evenings, our knees touching, while she told me the stories of her life. When I realised what she had been through, surviving two World Wars, losing her husband and two older children during these wars, and recently the final member of her immediate family, my father, I realised how relatively lucky I was to have a life with plenty of opportunities lying ahead of me.

Shortly after starting my job, we had a telephone installed so that I could be in touch with my grandmother during the day. She was enchanted by this piece of new technology, although it took me a while to explain to her how it worked. For quite some time, she kept holding it the wrong way around so that I could hear her, but she couldn't hear me because she was holding the microphone mouthpiece to her ear and the speaker to her mouth! This used to drive me crazy with frustration as I would be shouting down the phone, telling her to turn it around, but she couldn't hear me. She was also worried about ever missing a call, convinced that the phone would ring while she was in another room and she would miss it. She used to sit, staring at the phone, for hours on end, waiting for it to ring. But once she got the hang of it, she loved our phone conversations. She was very witty and had a great sense of humor, and I used to look forward to our daily phone conversations as much as she did.

My grandmother never failed to amaze me with her sharp mind and her robust physique. Even half way through her eighties, she was still as strong as an ox, carrying things around and cooking every day. Whenever I shared my fears about managing the bills and having to live on so little money, she simply said; "We will never starve while we have a little wheat and a garden." She showed me how to make her famous Tyrolean soup. Literally, you just fry two spoons of wheat in a pan until it starts to turn golden brown, then you pour in warm water and simmer it until it starts to thicken. Then, you add some salt and if you have some stale bread left over from the day before, you break it into pieces and add it to the soup, letting the liquid soak in. For our vegetables, we ate whatever we could find growing in the garden.

As a child, I had eaten my grandmother's famous wheat soup so many times, but now it took on a new meaning. Now, it suddenly symbolised the very act of survival. I still make it today, and I think fondly and proudly of my grandmother when I eat it. What I learnt from my grandmother is that there is always a solution to any problem in life. No matter how bad is the situation you are in, there is some way out if you look hard enough. Having never been to a doctor in her life, she also lived by the belief that there was no illness for which there was not an herb to cure it. She also always said that as long as you are alive, there is always a tomorrow with a new light, with new hope.

My job at the hotel was well paid but hardly stimulating for me, and it wasn't long before I felt bored and restless with it. I started applying for other, more ambitious jobs and I was extremely excited when, in January 1976, I saw an advertisement for what sounded like my dream job. The position was with an international tour operator based in Hannover, Northern Germany. They needed someone who spoke several languages, who was good in dealing with people and was able to handle unexpected challenges and new situations, to lead groups of tourists on specific organised tours around the world. I couldn't believe my luck when this international renowned company invited me to an interview; I felt as though the job was tailor made for me, as if it was what I had been born to do. All of a sudden, I remembered my vision when I was a teenager. I was literally over the moon when I received a job offer from them just a few weeks after the interview.

Coincidentally, my sister was planning to move back to Austria. She and her long-time boyfriend from the neighboring village were planning to get engaged. She had managed to transfer from her German college to a college in Salzburg to continue her nursing studies. We agreed that she and her boyfriend could live in the house rent-free on condition that they looked after our grandmother. This agreement suited us all; it really felt as though the stars had all lined up because everything worked out perfectly for everyone. I was able to leave and pursue my dream job while my sister and her boyfriend looked after our grandmother. They did so with great care and devotion, which was a huge relief to me. It also meant that we were able to fulfil our promise towards our grandmother. She was constantly in good hands and surrounded by her family until the very last moment of her life.

I still remember my grandmother's words she had said to me one evening during what has been our last evening together, while I was sitting at her bedside. She looked at me and gently whispered my name. Then, she longed for my hand, a thing she never had done before. She started telling me stories about her own life, about when she was young and about all the good things she remembered. As she kept telling me her stories, of which, most of them I knew already from before, she suddenly changed her voice and I could see tears in her glassy blue eyes. She paused for a moment, and then she said in the most loving tone; "Regina, I know you have the strength and courage to live your dream. You are still young, enjoy life and be always grateful for whatever life reveals to you." She continued saying that; "I had dreams too, however, these two World Wars have taken away all my dreams. The only dream that I kept dreaming of was finding a way to sustain myself and my children. However, there is one thing that life has taught me, and this is what I want you to understand too, because I know, that one day, you will remember and hold onto these words. No matter, what comes along your path, always keep 'looking up' and trust that only 'good' comes from up." By that, she wanted to tell me to stay optimistic and above all, have faith and trust in God, and know that He will never let me down because He loves me. Finally, she shared her last and only remaining wish with me. She folded her hands as if she was going to pray, she raised her eyes and then she slowly formulated the following words; "Please Lord, take me home, it's time for me to go." Her prayer has been heard, as two days later, on the 19th of December 1982, just before Christmas, and at the age of 91, she effortlessly passed away.

Today, 35 years later, I still believe that it was the most treasurable and valuable dowry my grandmother had given to me. She has always been and will always be my role model. My grandmother was a courageous and down to earth woman, a loving mother to her children, a caring housewife and a caretaker. But above all, she was a human being with an open heart, she is my all-time true heroine.

My new life, which was soon to be filled with plenty of exciting international travel, began in the beautiful Canary Islands where I completed an intense training course. After this, I was sent to southern Tunisia on my first assignment; it was a tough destination, but it promised to be a great adventure and I had always thrived on adventure; it was the reason I had applied for the job, after all. This was all so much more exciting than sitting behind the desk of a hotel reception in Austria.

I was filled with excitement and anxiety as I set off with my group of nine people, all from different destinations, speaking many different languages, on the first organised trip of my Tunisian posting. It was a camel trek across the *Chott el Djerid*, the biggest Salt Lake in the Sahara Desert. Our local guide was a man called Moustafa, who was of an indeterminate age. He could have been in his forties, he could have been in his seventies; it was impossible to tell. All I remember clearly is that he had only the front teeth left in his mouth. He had two large white front teeth in the middle of a face that was otherwise as black as ink. He also had a mischievous sense of humor. He made a kind of a joke by telling us that the translation for "Sahara" means "sand in your knickers" and that we were going to have a traditional Saharan barbecue. He told us that the location of this barbeque was in "the middle of nowhere." We were going to travel there on camels, and we were given special cushions to sit on atop these camels. We were also given traditional Arabian capes that were to protect us against the cold at night, and turbans to wear during the day to protect our heads from the scorching sun. The temperature drops quite sharply out in the desert as there is no cloud cover, but this also means that a full canopy of stars is visible every night, which is a beautiful sight to behold. There was a particularly romantic atmosphere at night during our trip as we were blessed with a full moon on the first night.

When we reached our destination for our "traditional Saharan barbecue" (which really was in the middle of nowhere), we discovered that the food on the menu was actually camel meat. The first taste of it was quite pleasant and sweet, but after chewing it for a while, we realised that it was absolutely impossible to swallow. We chewed and chewed and nothing happened. Honestly, it was like chewing on the rubber sole of a shoe. Only creatures with throats the size of elephants can swallow such kind of meat. We all exchanged pained looks as we tried and failed to swallow the meat. We were soon reaching for a drink to help us get the camel meat down. Each of us had been allocated a ration of five liters of water a day. We were instructed to drink three liters and use the remaining two to wash with. However, we were also given what felt like an unlimited supply of palm wine, and it was this drink that Moustafa offered us to go with our camel meat. This wine was extremely potent and no doubt, we were going to be the butt of another of Moustafa's jokes as we got steadily inebriated on it. Before we had drunk too much of the palm wine, Moustafa lined the camels up and then made them sit down in the sand. He directed us to sit in front of the camels and use them as our backrests (accurately anticipating that, with all the palm wine, we would not be able to sit upright for long). Camels had been our transportation, our dinner and now our furniture!

Not long after, Moustafa began to sing to us. He began to sing the French song "*Frère Jacques*." It turned out it was the only song he knew because he made us sing it every night. He tried to make us sing it in a round, but we soon got completely confused, which was hilariously funny at the time, and it wasn't long before we were literally passing out from the effects of this Saharan palm wine!

The year in Tunisia kicked off as one of the happiest and most exciting periods of my life, and even as I completed that one-year assignment, I thought back to how I had felt when I had left

Paris a year beforehand. How I had prayed that there was something good in store for me to compensate for the huge sacrifice I was making by giving up my studies. I realised that this was it, my dream job. Suddenly, my life was becoming an exciting adventure beyond my wildest dreams.

I grew to love my job that was, without doubt, the most wonderful reward for everything I had sacrificed when I had left Paris. I began traveling the world, visiting all these exotic places and meeting so many interesting people along the way. Over the next nearly eleven years, I traveled all around the world. I was sent to Mexico, Thailand, Singapore, Nepal, Malaysia, Spain, Haiti, Jamaica and the Canary Islands. Eventually, in January 1983, I was sent on a "short" mission to Cyprus that was supposed to be a six-week assignment, before going to India, to cover for another colleague who was based there and was taking some time off. At first, I had absolutely no idea where this place was and the only thing I knew was that my destination was the Greek side and that the people there only spoke Greek. While waiting for the doors of the airplane to open, there was nothing in the air to make me suspect that this trip would be any different from all the others I had made so far in my life. I still remember hearing someone behind me saying to his friend; "one-time Cyprus, always Cyprus." At this moment, I couldn't figure out what he meant, and as innocent as I was, I also couldn't have imagined that there would be anything so special about this trip, but indeed, there was!

Cyprus. Despite I had never heard of this Mediterranean island before, I was sent there, but that didn't make it any less attractive to me. In fact, I always relished the challenge of exploring new places, learning new languages and investigating new cultures.

I landed at Larnaca International Airport on the 1st of January 1983. Previously it was a military airport that had been used by the British Armed Forces since the 1930s. Larnaca Airport was quickly turned into the main international airport for the country, after the Turkish invasion in July 1974, which forced the closure of the original international airport in Nicosia; as a result, the facilities were still rather basic. I have a vivid memory, one that has never left me, of being engulfed in a warm, soft, sweet-tasting air that I had never before experienced, as soon as the doors of the airplane opened. I immediately felt as if this island had something mysterious about it, as if there was something magical in the air that was completely different from all the other islands I had visited. All of a sudden, I remembered the words the man in the airplane behind me had said to his friend. I had been to the Greek islands only once, so everything was new to me, the language, the traditions, the culture, the mentality. However, what captivated me the most was the enchanting mythology surrounding the island of Cyprus.

Cyprus (known in mythology as "Kypros") is also believed to be the "island of love." According to the Greek mythology, the goddess of love, Aphrodite, was born in Cyprus, actually by emerging from the sea at *Petra tou Romiou*, which is why this rock stack is known as "Aphrodite's Rock."

My new assignment was situated in the state of Paphos, on the southwest coast of the island. When I arrived in Paphos, there were only twenty-eight-thousand inhabitants. Paphos was surrounded by many hillside villages, where the traditional rural life was still thriving. The city centre itself was still growing. When I first arrived, there were four hotels; today there are more than fifty. My apartment (in a building that is still standing, although now surrounded by more modern developments) was only a few blocks away from the beach. When I first moved in, I didn't have too many neighbours; whereas now, my old home finds itself in the heart of one of the busiest tourist areas in Paphos.

I really enjoyed my first few weeks in Cyprus. I was kept busy organizing tailor-made excursions for customers, and I made time to soak up the local history and learn about the Cypriot traditions, but as with any other job I did, I knew I would be moving on after the six-week assignment ended. That's what I expected, anyway. Life, however, had other plans for me, plans that had all the makings of a Greek drama, which started, naturally, with an authentic love story "à la Méditerranée"!

By the beginning of February, when I had been living in Cyprus for just over a month, I had made a few local friends, and one of them invited me to a big party.

The guests were mostly Cypriot couples, with a few single locals and foreigners thrown in for good measure. People were kind enough to speak English with me, since, although I had picked up a little Greek by then, I still didn't know enough to hold a decent conversation. I had been impressed that most people in Cyprus I had met spoke enough English to hold a conversation. The music was mostly traditional Greek songs, and I was told a few of them were Cypriot ones. A group of men showed off their dancing skills, performing some of the island's most famous traditional Greek dances such as the *Sirtaki*, which I had learnt in Paris, the *Kalamatianos* and the *Zeimpekiko*.

We were served traditional Cypriot dishes, such as *Souvla* (grilled chicken and lamb), *Koupepia* (rice stuffed vine leaves),

Makaronia tou Fournou (an oven-baked macaroni dish) and a delicious Cypriot salad made with plenty of local olive oil and feta cheese. There was plenty of wine, all of it coming from local Cypriot villages. We were also served *Zivania*, a pomace brandy similar to grappa.

I remember the first part of the evening so clearly; it was filled with joy, laughter, great food, plenty of wine and impressive dancing. Then, out of the blue, I met the person who was destined to completely change the course of my life.

When my host introduced me to his friend, my first thought was; "Where have I met him before?" He looked so familiar to me, this tall, handsome man in his thirties who had just arrived at the party. I knew I hadn't actually met him before, but I couldn't shake the feeling that I had. Although Greek was obviously his mother tongue, he spoke English and German (my mother tongue) very well; it was unusual to find a German-speaking Cypriot, so this impressed me. We spoke in a mix of English and German.

When I asked my new companion his name, he answered: "Adonis."

I laughed and said I was honored to meet the "Greek God of Love." Then he asked my name and, just for fun, I replied:

"My name is Aphrodite."

We laughed together and again, I was struck by the feeling that, surely, I had met him before, almost as if I had known him for some time. I kept asking myself; *"Where do I know him from?"* I felt like I had known him for years and even though we didn't speak the same mother tongue, and still, it felt as if somehow, we were speaking the same unique language. All I knew was that I had to keep talking to this man. I felt so curious about him; I wanted to explore everything about him. I was quite transfixed by him. Whatever these feelings were, I honestly had never felt anything so powerful in all my life. I really did feel as if the "God of Love" was standing before me. I couldn't stop staring into his huge and sparking green eyes; I had never seen eyes that were such an intense green color. He couldn't take his eyes off me either!

We had become so absorbed in our conversation that we didn't notice the time passing, and at one point, I looked up and saw that almost everyone had left the party. We were amongst the last remaining guests. I thought I better wrap up the conversation and I began to thank him for such a wonderful time, because I had really enjoyed his company. I couldn't even finish my sentence before he took my hand, kissed it gently, and asked if he could see me again soon. I was enveloped in the warmest feeling I had ever experienced; I felt like I had been touched by love. I can't remember exactly how I responded, but I do recall thinking that my words didn't matter because I knew he understood everything I felt from how I was looking at him. He said that he wanted to show me where "I" (Aphrodite) was born, according to the Greek mythology. So, we made arrangements as to where and when to meet a few days later and then went our separate ways.

I couldn't sleep for two nights, as thoughts of the "Greek God" I met, kept swirling around in my mind. I couldn't wait until I saw him again. When I look back now, I still remember every single moment of our first real date together. I will never forget it!

Adonis had told me to meet him down by the Paphos harbour, what is now the main tourist meeting point of the town was then a sea wall with a few fishing boats moored to it. There was one tiny kiosk that sold a few refreshments, whereas now there are tenths of little shops and restaurants, serving the locals and tourists all year round. The only thing that hasn't changed in all that time is the view of the old castle (Medieval Fort) that stands at the edge of the harbour and is an iconic landmark of the area.

I set off from my apartment and began to walk through the field that ran along the coast, towards the harbour. I passed the rusted chassis of an old village bus that had apparently been there for as long as anyone could remember. It was something of a quirky local point of interest, and there was usually a family of goats chewing at the patches of grass that grew around and under it.

As I walked, I noticed every single thing around me, as if all my senses had been attuned. The late afternoon sun was still warm and I could smell the intense perfume of the flowering almond trees that lined the roadside. I could hear the waves below me, breaking on the rocks. Everywhere I looked, I saw *Cyclamens* (the national flower of Cyprus, a protected species of flora and a local traditional symbol of true love) blooming in all their glorious shades of pink, purple and red.

I came to the main coastal road and started heading towards the Medieval Fort, which I could see in the distance. That was where Adonis had told me to meet him. I was sure that he had clearly seen me, and perhaps he was too impatient because long before I reached our appointed meeting place, a car pulled up beside me, a door opened and the "love of my life" stepped out, holding in his hands, a single red rose.

This beautiful "God of Love" slowly approached me without saying a word; he simply smiled at me, as if he was feeling the most intense joy. When he was close by, he gently handed me the rose. He then took my hands, looked deep into my eyes and said in the softest, most tender and loving voice; "My love, I have been waiting for you for so long and finally, I have found you."

We embraced each other, and although we stood in the peaceful silence of love. If that silence could have spoken for me, it would have said; "You are my 'Great Love' and I will follow you wherever you take me." Huge, overwhelming feelings of love engulfed us, and I didn't doubt, for one moment, that I was at the doorstep of a new life, all of which I was ready to spend with this man.

Eventually we returned to the car and drove to the place he so wanted to show me. I had seen Aphrodite's Rock before from the road, but this was the first time I was going to see it from up close.

When we arrived, the sun had already gone down and the full moon had come out, making the whole scene even more magical and romantic. We carefully climbed down the rocks with the moonlight being bright enough to light our way. I felt as though I was about to experience something unique, something that was of a great privilege.

We walked across the pebbled beach towards the rock that looked majestic in the moonlight, with the starry sky as its backdrop. Adonis told me to lean up against its gently sloping sides, as this was apparently the way how you feel the rock's divine energy. I pressed my body into this rock and felt my skin tingle with electricity. I had never felt anything so powerful in nature before.

After a good length of time spent absorbing the powerful energy that radiated from this ancient rock, my "Love" took my hand and led me down to the shore, where we started to walk. We walked for what felt like, at the same time, hours and hours or just a few seconds, because it was as if time had no more meaning; what we had found together felt timeless and endless. We didn't see another soul on our walk and we spoke few words. We simply walked, with the sound of the waves lapping the shore and the crunch of the pebbles under our feet providing us with a soundtrack, as though we were the only creatures in existence. To date, I have never experienced, or been able to imagine, anything more romantic as this first night we spent together at that magical spot. I felt at peace, as if I was giving in to the will of the universe and therefore everything would happen exactly as it should from this moment on.

Our night at Aphrodite's Rock marked the beginning of a lifelong, loving union between Adonis and me. We were old enough to understand what to expect and what life really meant to us. We agreed to give this relationship enough time to grow, and to allow it to develop a solid foundation, strong enough to support a future family life together. Even though it was hard to resist against the physical desire of intimacy, we both knew that if we patiently waited for things to develop naturally, this would only enhance the quality of our relationship, a thing we both aimed for. We believed that 'marriage' meant something unique and holy, and at the time we didn't feel ready for that step. However, during the first two years of our relationship, we had plenty of opportunities to discover each other on a deeper level. During that period, we actually never discussed our practical arrangements in much detail, we just made suggestions, amicably agreed plans and then went along with them. We dearly loved and enjoyed life together. Neither did we feel obliged to follow anyone else's opinions, nor traditions. Eventually, we became aware that the depth of our love was all we needed to keep us bonded together, and what will continue to nurture our union, just like the flame of a candle that never extinguishes. Few years later, we both knew and strongly felt that it was time for us to take the next step ahead. Within Adonis' community, it was rather odd for a man at his age not to get married straight away.

Adonis was born in a small village located in the hillside above Paphos. He came from a large local Cypriot family, the fourth of eight children (three boys and five girls in total). As an adult, he became widely known throughout Cyprus for being a dynamic and successful entrepreneur. He was highly respected and popular within the local society, and he was known for his open heart and deep generosity towards those who were less fortunate than he was. Everyone seemed to know him; he was the heart and soul of the party wherever he went.

To begin with, I was genuinely surprised to discover how different Adonis' family was from him. They seemed introverted and closed-minded. I tried to get to know them and make friends with them, but I think they found me too exuberant and opinionated. I was also an outsider, a foreigner, and I began to suspect that this might have contributed to their wariness of me, as if they had an inherent mistrust of foreigners.

The girls in the family had been raised according to the family's rural traditions. There were five of them and the oldest two had been sent out to work in the fields after receiving a very basic education, only completing elementary school. The family's tradition dictated that the men in the family were responsible for finding husbands for their sisters. I was shocked to witness the way in which the women were bound to the men of the family; they were expected to adhere to the will of their husbands and brothers without question. In particular, the men controlled the finances and the women were expected to ask for any money they needed, even for some new clothes or toiletries for themselves.

For me, an extremely independent woman who had been making her own money and paying her own way since I was a teenager, this was difficult to understand. Adonis and I obviously didn't operate this way and he always respected the fact that I had a career and was self-supporting.

Another tradition Adonis' family adhered to stated that the men could not get married until all of their sisters were married off, and although four of the girls were already married, the fifth one was not. In a perverse way, this gave us the technical excuse to live together before marriage.

Adonis had two brothers who couldn't have been more unlike him. The eldest one, Draco, never spoke to me. I had never met anyone so unfriendly. I never saw him smile and hardly ever heard him speak. I couldn't work out if it was me whom he disliked, or just life in general. He certainly seemed to be deeply unhappy. The younger one, Kyriakos, was slightly more forthcoming, but only in perfunctory way; I never felt any warmth from him either. With a hindsight, I suspected that they were angry that Adonis wasn't getting married to a local Cypriot woman. I think they may have resented him for flying in the face of their strong sense of tradition. Also, there was possibly some jealousy regarding all the business success Adonis had achieved. In fact, I uncovered evidence to support this theory a few years down the line.

It's not as if the brothers hadn't enjoyed some success of their own. Adonis had encouraged his younger brother, Kyriakos, to study finance and seek a position at the local bank. Kyriakos had risen to the highly respectable position of a bank manager. The older brother, Draco, was working for Adonis by the time I came on the scene, but he had reportedly once worked for the Criminal Investigation Department in Nicosia. Although no one knew for sure, what exactly he had done there because he had always been so mysterious about it. Neither of Adonis' brother seemed to have any great ambition, but I can imagine how hard it must have been to live in Adonis' shadow, the pioneering successful businessman with a huge personality.

I always felt it was a shame that Adonis' siblings didn't gain inspiration from their brother's open-minded attitude and worldliness; it was as if they pointedly resisted his inquisitive, explorative nature, even resented it. In turn, Adonis became disinterested in their opinions and seemed to deal with them in an almost disassociated manner.

But what his family seemed to lack in warmth for me, his friends certainly made up for it.

One day, only a few weeks after we had met, Adonis was due to pick me up for a date and he was unusually late. Although most Cypriot people I had met were very poor timekeepers, Adonis, like me, was more like the northern Europeans; like the Germans, he was very strict on punctuality. So, when he was late on this particular occasion, I began to get worried. Young people these days, with their instant communication on mobile phones, have no idea what it used to feel like when you had no way of contacting someone to let them know you were going to be late, or to chase someone up to find out where they had got up to.

The minutes ticked by and I was getting rather annoyed with my new "aficionado." Finally, there was a knock at the door. I opened it and found, not one, but two men, standing at the door of my apartment. Adonis introduced his friend Nikos to me, and then said something to him in Greek. Nikos looked at me from up to down, slowly, then he replied in Greek. Adonis smiled and nodded. My Greek was still very basic then and I didn't know what they had said to each other. Years later, I found out what that interchange had been all about.

Adonis cared about no one's opinion except that of his best friend, Nikos. He had told Nikos he had fallen in love with a girl and wanted to know what Nikos thought of her. When they arrived at my place, Adonis had simply said; "So, what do you think?" Nikos had replied; "Yes, you in the end found her! So, what are you waiting for? Get on with it!"

Nikos and his wife, Maria, became great friends of mine too. Every weekend we would go out dancing with them at some traditional taverns in one of the many beautiful villages surrounding Paphos. We would have so much fun. There were always several bottles of wine open wherever we went. We would sit at the outside tables and the men would invite anyone who walked past to come and join us. All passers-by were invited to join us at our table, to enjoy a glass of wine with us, and join in with the dancing and laughter.

I got to hear many interesting and entertaining stories from Nikos, some of which really helped me gain a picture of who Adonis had been as a young man. He clearly had a colorful history.

One story, I always remember was the one featuring Tsestos. Tsestos was the village "idiot." When he was at school, he managed to pass the first three classes of primary school before he took on all sorts of jobs in the village. He never got married, and everyone in the village loved him because of his funny sense of humor.

During the Turkish invasion of 1974, there were rumors of local people stealing weapons from the Cypriot army's military base. Various individuals came under suspicion, although no one seemed to know who the real traitors were.

Nikos and Maria were living in Limassol at the time, and one evening they were driving home after a dinner in Paphos. They decided to take a detour through the village where Nikos had grown up. As they drove up the steep road leading into the village, they saw an old man stumbling up the hill. Nikos immediately knew exactly who it was; it was Tsestos, the village drunk. Nikos pulled up alongside him, wanting to make sure he was okay. He leaned out of the window to speak to the old man and found that he was muttering about this crime, about the weapons that had been stolen. Nikos decided to tease him and said; "Tsestos, Tsestos, what's going on? Do you know who stole these weapons? Tell me! Wait, let me write down their names and I will punish them all," Nikos said to him.

Tsestos looked at him and then said; "Why are you asking me? I am a small fry. Why ask me when your best friend is the top dog, the big cheese, the guy who knows everything about everyone?!"

He was referring to Adonis.

When he was telling me this story, Nikos assured me that, however drunk Tsestos got, he never lost his mind, he was always logical and knew exactly what he was talking about. This gave me a great image of who Adonis was and how he was perceived locally.

I heard many more stories about my new "Love," especially about some of his wild and crazy adventures; it seemed as though the whole village worried about Adonis; was he ever going to settle down? He was a wild one; not in a destructive way, but if he thought of doing something, he would do it, no matter what it took to get it. If there was something he wanted (a piece of land, a new business… a girl) he would go all out and get it. There was an untamed, childlike quality to him. Perhaps, what he was definitely waiting for was a charming and strong-minded "Austrian" girl to come along and drag him into adulthood!

After meeting Adonis, I obviously decided to stay in Cyprus. My company told me that while they would always be happy to hire me during the peak tourist season, they would not necessarily be able to offer me work during the winter months; I would have to find my own work during that time.

I managed to get a regular job at a big four-star hotel along the seafront. In these days, it was the only four-star hotel in Paphos, and it was called the "Paphos Beach Hotel," which years later it became the "Almyra Hotel." I was responsible for organising entertainment programs for the long-stay guests, those who came over to Cyprus from northern Europe, in order to get some winter sun. One year, I organised a big water polo tournament between the locals and the visitors. Random people still approach me to this day, saying that they still remember me organizing such events!

Towards the end of 1986, when we had been together for three and a half years, I became pregnant for the first time. Adonis and I discussed our present situation, and we've decided to give up my job and raise a big family. He was more than happy about this, so I gave notice to my company. As a parting gift for my hard work and ten years of service, the company offered me two airplane tickets to anywhere in the world we would like to go. Actually, Adonis and I always wanted to visit the United States of America, so we booked our flights to New York. Sadly, that first pregnancy ended with a miscarriage, but we had our trip booked, so we had something wonderful to look forward to.

A few months before we left, I remember receiving my final pay slip from my company; it arrived one morning in the middle of November. I opened it and left it on the coffee table without thinking. When Adonis came home from work, he saw it. Looking at the figure, he asked me if it was my pay slip for three or six months. No, I replied, it was just for one month. As he had never asked me how much money I earned, I think he was shocked. He told me that even the top hotel managers in Paphos didn't earn that much per month. He then asked me, either out of fun or serious, I never really knew, if I was really sure I wanted to give up my job to raise our children, because with that money we could have a nice life if we combined our earnings!

I didn't take the decision to resign from my well-paid job lightly. I was aware that I would become totally financially dependent on Adonis. I even remember buying a really nice winter coat for our upcoming trip to the U.S.A. and thinking to myself, I wonder if this is the last big purchase I will make with my own money. In the more than three years we had been together, Adonis couldn't have been more generous and I didn't doubt his commitment to me for one second, but it was still a gamble. Who knew what could happen on this island, where I was still a foreigner. Somewhere inside I reassured myself, however, that if something really bad happened, I could always return to Austria or Germany. Maybe my old company would even give me my job back. But for the time being, I put all the "eggs" in my "God of Love's" basket and went along with the plan.

In February 1987, after having known each other for four years, we set off on the trip of a lifetime that began in New York City.

Arriving at the John F. Kennedy (JFK) Airport in New York was a significant moment for me. I belong to the generation most of whom remember exactly the date when U.S. President Kennedy was shot. This tragedy made a huge impression on me. I felt as though I was connected to John F. Kennedy in a significant way. We didn't own a television in Austria in the 1960s, but our neighbors had one. My siblings and I were occasionally invited over to watch some kids' TV programs, which was always an exciting occasion and a big treat. But nothing could have prepared us for what we witnessed on our TV screens on the 22nd of November 1963. I was only eleven years old at the time, but somehow, I felt the impact of the assassination deeply. I was acutely aware that the world had lost a very special soul. As I watched the funeral, I felt like I had a huge attachment to this man and as though I was actually present at the event. To this day, I can still vividly picture it in my mind. So, when I arrived at JFK Airport twenty-four years later, I felt a jolt of excitement. There was a specific energy around me; I knew I was meant to be here.

For four days, we walked everywhere, taking in all the great, iconic Manhattan sights such as the Empire State Building, the World Trade Center, and the place that meant the most to me, the Statue of Liberty. The Statue of Liberty was erected in New York Harbour at the end of the 19th century to welcome all the immigrants who arrived in the United States. I identified with those early settlers, people who left their homeland and made a new base in a foreign land.

We stayed at the Lexington Hotel on Lexington Avenue, close to Grand Central Station. We had not been aware when we had booked it, that the hotel was a favorite haunt of Rauf Raif Denktaş. Denktaş was the founding President of Northern Cyprus (the northern part of Cyprus that is recognised as an independent state by Turkey and as the "Turkish-occupied territory of the Republic of Cyprus" by the international community). He often held meetings with the then President of Cyprus,

Spyros Kyprianou, at the Lexington Hotel to discuss the future of Cyprus. We discovered this information when we checked out of the hotel because we were told that Denktaş had been staying there at the same time. We had literally been sleeping with the "enemy!"

Our next stop was Washington D.C. and we obviously had to kick off our sightseeing expedition by visiting John F. Kennedy's humble grave, where a single flame burns on a flat memorial stone. The other monuments and famous buildings in Washington were impressive, but nothing meant as much to me as seeing Kennedy's grave.

Our favorite city was, without doubt, San Francisco. We loved everything about it. There was drama and romance in the undulating streets and unique architecture. There was something rather European about it. The city seemed to have its own identity that set it apart from all the grandeur we had witnessed in the U.S.A. up to that point. The history of the city was fascinating, and we loved the beauty of the surrounding natural environment.

From San Francisco, we traveled to Los Angeles, where I remember walking for hours up and down identical-looking streets. We also stayed in a rather grand hotel downtown that was miles away (in distance and feeling) from the usual tourist spots like Beverly Hills, Santa Monica, Disneyland and the Hollywood Studios. That hotel will always have a special significance for me because it was where we conceived our second child, our first son, Markos!

From Los Angeles, we flew to Las Vegas, which really was like nothing I had ever seen in my life. We got into a taxi at the airport and asked the driver to show us around. He drove down a long straight road that was lined on both sides with gigantic hotels; it honestly looked as though we had been shrunk and the world around us had become supersized. When we finally got to the end of "the strip," there was nothing, nothing at all, just vast stretches of sand with mountains in the distance. It really was simply a city in the middle of nowhere, in the middle of a massive desert.

We got tickets to the famous Siegfried and Roy show. Those white lions and white tigers were astonishing; I had never seen anything like it in my life. But more mesmerising sights were in store for us when we arrived at the Grand Canyon. Only those who have witnessed this great sight, one of the seven natural wonders of the world, will appreciate the feelings we had when we saw it. The experience was a shared treasure moment for us as a couple, and especially the flying tour in and along the Grand Canyon.

Our final destination was Florida. We flew to Orlando, rented a car and drove to Daytona Beach, where the famous car rallies are held.

On our last day, we set off for Miami Airport where we were due to board our flight back to Cyprus. We had no idea that it was nearly 300 miles away, and therefore the drive was going to be around eight hours. We found ourselves on a long, straight road, with nothing on either side of us; no turns, no gas stations, literally nothing! We grew increasingly anxious about the possibility of breaking down, and as time dragged on, with no sign of Miami Airport in the distance, we actually began to worry that we might miss our flight. At one point, we joked that we should perhaps keep driving south and take a boat to Cuba. Of course, we didn't, but it was in that moment that we agreed Cuba would be our next "big trip."

Little did we know then that we had just completed our one and only "big trip" as a couple because in nine months' time, we were going to welcome the first addition to what was set to become a rather large family. There would be no more big travels for me for many years; I was imminently to become immersed in motherhood!

Year 1987. Our lives took on a new direction on the 10th of November 1987, when I gave birth to our first child; our son, Markos. The moment we held our precious boy in our arms, we knew it was the most significant experience of our lives.

We were still living in my little beachfront apartment at that point and were rapidly growing out of it, so we bought a slightly larger apartment over on the other side of the town with the intention of purchasing a larger house in a nearby village in the coming years.

Before Markos' birth, we had been real social butterflies; while after his birth, Adonis assumed we would soon go back to our old lifestyle. I think he got a bit of a shock when I explained that those days were over. He suggested we leave the baby with his sister whenever we wanted to go out, but this wasn't acceptable to me. Eventually, he began to understand that life had changed, but also that the precious new life was giving us far more joy than a lifetime of partying.

I didn't slip seamlessly into my new roles either; it also took me some time to adjust. Until I met Adonis, I had been a highly independent woman. Ever since my parents died, I had not had the time or desire for big love affairs; I had been completely focused on building my career; I was a single, working, independent woman. I was simply "Regina," my own woman, a career driven woman, a well-traveled adventurer.

I had coped with many changes in my life before, but motherhood was probably the biggest shift. I had to go from taking care of only me, to taking care of a family of three. I had to redefine myself, taking on the role of a devoted partner and mother. I loved every moment of it, but I did sacrifice my freedom, and that wasn't easy to get used to. There were also issues for Adonis and I to overcome, relating to our very different cultural backgrounds and the contrasting ways in which we had been raised, as is often the case with couples who have different nationalities. But the strong bond of our love got us through the up and downs. I never regretted my decision; it was simply a new path, a hard one, but one that was endlessly rewarding.

Over the next six years, I gave birth to four more children. Eva was born in January 1989, Diogenis in June 1990, Adonis Jr. in March 1992 and finally Cleopatra in July 1993. Those who knew us often commented on what a close-knit family we were, and complimented Adonis and I on how we were raising our children to be so loving and caring of each other. We were extremely sociable; but in a different way unlike before, now we loved to entertain and regularly welcomed guests into our home.

Shortly after the birth of our second child, Eva, we found a property in a small village a few minutes' drive in-land from Paphos city centre. The house was perfect for us to grow in and build on. A generous piece of land surrounded it, and we set about cultivating this in order to plant several varieties of vegetables and fruits. We had enough room to keep chickens and a whole range of other domesticated farm animals. We really had everything we needed; it was a joy to watch our children grow up in a house filled with love, laughter and healthy food.

Around the same time as we were buying the house, we finally got married in church. In fact, we had waited for the last of Adonis' sisters to be married before we went ahead with our nuptials. In the end, it was a very quick, simple church ceremony. We scheduled it for the same day as Eva's christening, so that our families were already assembled. We hired the church for the christening and asked the priest to stay on for another hour and to marry us. We were extremely excited to receive the blessings and to seal our loving bond in front of God, but we also did it for the sake of our children. I'm also glad Adonis' mother saw us get married; she sadly died two months later, on Markos' second birthday.

The eighth member of our family was our dog Lassie, a female Collie, just like the one in the TV show that the children loved to watch. She was fiercely protective of the children, the guardian of our family and home. I never worried about the children when they were playing outside because Lassie was always by their side and would never have let anyone come near them without her permission. She even protected them from me, growling at me on the odd occasion when I had to raise my voice to the children when they misbehaved!

Lassie was the chief, but I had a whole menagerie of animals to look after. We had parrots, ducks, geese, cats and rabbits as pets. We even had a peacock that strutted about the yard displaying his colorful tail feathers. Then there were the chickens that we kept, providing us with eggs. The children would sit for hours waiting for the hens to lay their eggs; they took great pleasure from watching some of those hens sit on the eggs until they hatched into baby chicks.

I will never forget the time when Adonis Jr. got concerned because one of the chickens hadn't laid an egg for several days. He had announced his intention to become a veterinarian when he was older and decided to get some early experience by giving the chicken a helping hand. He picked up this particular chicken and thrust his fingers into the hole where he expected the egg to be hiding. All he got was a handful of chicken poo! Disgusted, he dropped the chicken and went to wash himself off under the garden tap. Undeterred, he returned to re-inspect the animal, lifting her high above his head, trying to see what was going on in her nether regions. At that moment, the chicken decided to play ball and laid an egg... right on top of Adonis Jr.'s head! It cracked and the raw egg ran down his face. That was the end of his fledgling veterinary career.

My greatest ambition was to be self-sufficient, so I worked hard to grow all of our own food. I was also keen to teach the children where their food came from. I remember friends of theirs coming for dinner and seeing all of our plants, and then asking where were the "tomato plants." They were looking for plants with tomatoes, alongside other trees growing other fruits, because they didn't understand how tomatoes grew. Our children knew where everything came from.

Adonis and I, we always impressed the children with how lucky they were to be living in such a beautiful country. Cyprus is an idyllic place to grow up, with so much natural beauty surrounding you. We added to this by creating a real sanctuary of nature on our property, with different sections for growing fruits and vegetables and a large separate area for the animals. We also owned some land near the Paphos Airport on which we had planted an orchard before the children were born. We had over three hundred trees that consisted of oranges, lemons, apples, pears, grapefruits and avocados. Our diet throughout the year included whatever was in season.

Cyprus is a magical country. Adonis would always tell us that if you are starving in Cyprus then you are lazy. The country has abundant fresh produce that grows wild all over the island. Potatoes, and many kinds of vegetables, and fresh fruits, are all readily available, often for nothing. You can live on practically anything! And the good weather means you can live in the humblest of dwellings because you will never be too cold. You need very little to live a healthy life in Cyprus.

The children had plenty of space to play in. They ran around in the garden and played many games like hide-and-seek or catch, weaving in and out of the fruit trees. At the very bottom of the garden, they had a little wooden house where they would hang out for hours on end. With around three-hundred days a year of sunshine in Cyprus, they were lucky enough to live in a place where they could spend at least ten months of the year playing outdoors (in stark contrast to my childhood that had been filled with so many dark and cold winter days). They had many adventures in their own back garden and experienced the ups and downs of life in a relatively safe environment.

I always felt fortunate to be able to give my children such a warm and comfortable home. I relished the early years of their childhood; I showered them with love and taught them as much as I could. I believe a child's first few years are so formative and vitally important. Therefore, I wanted my children to feel safe and protected, but also to have space to explore, ask questions and discover life for themselves. You only have one chance to give a child a good foundation and the right start in life, so I dedicated myself to ensuring our children had plenty of quality time with their parents and that they experienced the healthiest life we could offer them.

There were many times during my first few years of marriage and motherhood when I stopped and marveled at what a wonderful life I had, and asked myself if, perhaps it was all "too good to be true." I only wished my parents had lived to see the life I had created on the beautiful island of Cyprus.

I never missed my mother as much as I did during my first pregnancy. I desperately wished she was still alive. She had taught me so many things throughout my life, but we had never spoken in any detail about pregnancy and childbirth. Eventually, I found something of a mother substitute in Sheila Kitzinger.

Sheila was a British author, a natural birth activist who wrote books on pregnancy and childbirth. I responded to the practical yet motherly tone in her book. I practiced her prenatal exercises and followed all her advice. Her books resonated to me as if she was truly like a mother to me. In Cyprus, in 1987, I didn't come across anyone willing to talk about pregnancy issues. I felt very alone; the female members of Adonis' family did not seem to want to play that motherly role for me. Sheila was my mother-from-afar, a kindred soul who, coincidentally, had also had five children of her own.

I read all Sheila's advice about raising children, and I also added to it whatever I remembered from my own upbringing.

I tried to second-guess what my wise mother would have told me if she was alive. In particular, I wanted to ensure that, even from a young age, each of my children understood the value of things and their responsibilities in life. Everyone had daily tasks. From the age of around four or five years old, the children took on age-appropriate chores around the house. There was the feeding of and caring for the animals, the cleaning of their cages, and various other small jobs around the garden and inside the house, to be done. When I told people that we managed the house, the garden, the animals and all the children with no outside help of any kind, they hardly ever believed me. They couldn't imagine how it could be done. But we did it, with the help of a strictly-organised program. We had a weekly chart that showed who should be doing what and when. Once the children had finished their chores, they were free to go and play. These were mostly simple tasks, such as sweeping up leaves, or feeding the chickens, or picking vegetables, but everyone had to do their part to contribute to the running of the household. I wanted them to remember that we were a family; a united team.

The children were rewarded for completing their tasks. I had a system that awarded them various points for each task and we totaled them all up on a Saturday (the day when they all had to clean their own rooms thoroughly). They earned rewards for reaching a certain number of points. The size and type of reward would also be dependent on their age; it was usually something like an ice-cream, or some sweets, or a toy, or for the elder ones a movie ticket for the cinema.

With five children, my biggest concern was ensuring that they all felt they were being heard, that they all had a chance to speak up and have their fair say. I organised a meal roster so that each of them got to enjoy their favorite meal on one day a week. We always had our main meal for our lunch. We would start with some fresh salad from the garden and then there was a different main course each day. For example, spaghetti Bolognese on a Monday, chicken "al Forno" on a Tuesday, grilled fish on a Wednesday, etc. We ate our own grown vegetables with each main dish and always finished with some fruit or dessert.

We tried to eat our meals together as a family, in particular breakfast and lunch. Mealtimes were sociable times; we encouraged the children to express themselves and talk about whatever has happened during the day. Sometimes this would initiate big, long conversations, and there was always plenty of laughter. For dinner, they usually had a light evening meal and we finished off the day with a night prayer. After the children were all in bed sleeping, Adonis and I would eat something together, accompanied with a glass of wine and enjoy some precious moments alone. These moments were particularly important and appreciated, given the size of our large family; it was hard to get a moment's peace with so many energetic and intelligent young people constantly running through the house!

As soon as the children started school and began to learn how to read and write, I gave them weekly pocket money. I handed these out on Sunday evening. Each child had their money wrapped in an envelope with their name written on it. I also gave them each a notebook and showed them how to enter their income and expenditure in two separate columns, with the date written above, in order to teach them basic day-to-day accounting. Everything they bought got entered into the book. I remember secretly watching them when they thought I wasn't looking, trying to balance their books, sometimes hiding them under the table and whispering to each other things like; "Shall I just write down one more lollipop so that the money adds up?" I had to stop myself from laughing out loud.

The children knew that they had to buy some of their school supplies using their pocket money, so they had to allow for this before buying sweets or toys. I provided them with the basics and whatever they needed to eat at school, such as a sandwich, a snack or a juice, but if they needed an extra pencil or a notebook, they had to use their pocket money. Anything they didn't spend was put into their piggy bank as their savings. They would then use this money to buy special treats—like an ice-cream or a small souvenir—on our annual vacation, which usually took place on one of the Greek Islands.

Adonis and I both felt strongly that it was important to teach our children to appreciate the value of money from a young age. We encouraged them to consider carefully every purchase they wanted to make, to ensure they didn't waste money or spend too much on frivolous things. They learnt to save their money because they knew it didn't work by asking me for extra cash. If they had any legitimate expenses that their own pocket money couldn't cover, such as something they needed for a school project, then we would discuss it on Sunday evening. Together, we would then decide whether it was an exceptional necessity, and whether it was me the one responsible to buy it for them, or whether it was something they had to save for.

Each year, on their birthdays, the children received a raise in their pocket money, but this was conditional on an understanding about their clothing and shoeing requirements. When they were young, I had made most of their clothing myself. I did an evening class in sewing, and as a creative person, I really enjoyed making garments for all of them. But as they grew up and life got busier, I obviously had to start buying them clothes and shoes. Many of their friends were always wearing brand new, fashionable items, but I wanted our children to appreciate how expensive it would be if we were constantly buying these new fashionable items all the time, especially for a family with five children. So, I made a deal with them. I said that they could have their pocket money increase if they accepted the less expensive, more practical shoes and clothes that I would buy them. I told them that I had no objection if they wanted to save their pocket money and buy the more expensive ones, but that would take a longer time to save up. They gradually realised that the less expensive things did the job just as well as the expensive ones, and preferred to save their pocket money for other things. Even when they had some spare money saved up and wanted to spend it on clothes and shoes, they tended to buy the cheaper ones rather than use all their savings to buy the more expensive ones.

I always felt that one of the most important things I could teach our children was how to deal with money. By teaching them a basic accounting system, starting from a very early age, and helping them stick to it as they grew older, it has meant that they have all become responsible and sensible with money, with no financial problems. They are all good with money, and none of them is particularly bothered with fashion, like many of their contemporaries. They prefer to buy inexpensive practical clothes and make their money go further. They will spend on quality, but not on frivolous fashionable items that are overpriced. Another valuable lesson they learned while growing up was to support their siblings in terms of money. As for example, all the children contributed in their capacity for the teeth braces for the ones in need of.

There are many vital life lessons I feel I taught my children, but gratefulness, the appreciation of love, the importance of respect, and how to deal with money and other material things are probably the most important ones.

In 1995, in the summer before Markos was due to start school and when Cleopatra was fully mobile and able to communicate (having just turned two), I decided to take the children to Austria so they could learn a little about their mother's homeland. After all the years I had spent bringing up our children, I realised that I had not actually been on an airplane or made a big trip anywhere for about eight years since the trip to the U.S.A. that Adonis and I had taken in February 1987. I had itchy feet!

When I announced my plan, my husband thought I had gone crazy. He said I could certainly take them if I wanted to, if I felt I could cope with them, but that he would not be making that journey with us. He gave me his excuse by telling me that he was busy with work anyways and said that if we went, he could join us for a few days towards the end of the trip. He much feared that I would not be able to handle five children on my own.

And so, I got myself prepared for an international flight on my own with five children under eight years old. I made each of the children wear a little plastic pocket around their necks that contained their name, my name and our phone number, and about £20 (Cyprus Pounds). Once I was sure I had taken every precaution against losing any of my children, we set off on our travels.

The airplane journey itself was a great adventure. The three oldest children sat in one row and I sat across the aisle with the youngest two. As we were queuing up to get on board, I could feel people around us staring at us, probably praying they would not be sitting near us. Although the children were generally well-behaved, the noise level was always rather high; after all, the only way they knew how to have their own voice heard was to raise it. There was a cacophony of little voices calling; "Regina, Regina…" as they tried to get my attention.

(This was a little family quirk, that the children always called me "Regina." I don't know how it started, but I simply never instructed them not to. To this day, they all call me by my name. They only refer to me as their "mum" when they are talking about me amongst them or to someone else. Adonis and I thought it was charming, so we never stopped them. Thus, we continued our tradition of being the non-traditional family!)

As Markos was old enough, he was invited to visit the cockpit and meet the pilots; this was quite normal in those days. I remember how excited Markos was when he saw all the controls and spoke to the captain. I am sure this is what gave him his lifelong ambition to be a pilot after all.

We safely arrived at Vienna Airport in Austria and disembarked the airplane looking rather like the "von Trapp" family (musical TV show). We stayed with some wonderful old friends of mine, but I made sure we were only around for a short time each morning and evening. I didn't want their house to become too noisy. I made a busy daily program for the children that started at 7 a.m. and was so full of activity that, by the time we came home at 5 p.m. each evening, the only thing they had energy for was to have a quick shower, to eat a small supper, quietly, and go straight to bed. My goal was to wear them out each day, and it worked! My friends, our hosts, couldn't believe how well-behaved the children were; I explained that I simply made sure they had no energy for getting "too active." My husband was also greatly impressed with all the organisation and structure I had put into place when he joined us during the second week of our vacation there.

We did so much on that trip; we visited places in Austria that I had not even seen myself. We went on mountain treks in the countryside, visited museums, and took part in all kinds of traditional activities. We enjoyed it so much that we went back three summers in a row. However, I always remember that first summer with great fondness. I remember the relief I felt when I realised that my children were going to be great travelers. I knew, from that first trip, that I would always be able to travel with them. After that, we went on to visit many countries in Europe when they were still young. We went to the U.K., France, Italy, Spain, Greece and Germany. To this day, my children all have an insatiable appetite for travel.

I really had the picture-perfect life. The love between my husband and I continued to thrive, and we were proud of our healthy and intelligent children, who all excelled through their school years. Besides of looking after and taking care of my large family, I ran the household and one of our family businesses, and my husband continued with all his various commercial ventures. There were ups and downs, as there are in any family, and it was hard work, of course, but we couldn't have been happier. We had everything we needed and we treasured every moment of our privileged and blessed life.

Up to this point, you must have some clear idea of the beautiful picture that was shattered and came to an abrupt end one sunny Wednesday afternoon in February 2002. Towards the end of that particular sunny winter day, the life we knew and dearly loved had gone forever.

PART TWO

February 2002. My last goodbye to my love. I had first said hello to the love of my life in February 1983, so it was ironic that this was also the month in which I had to bid him goodbye, 19 years later.

It was Wednesday, 20th of February 2002, an unusually warm and sunny day for this time of winter season in Cyprus. I clearly remember it was "spaghetti day" and I have a vivid picture of the whole family eating spaghetti for lunch, gathered around the table in the room we called our "Pergola." Even though this was an enclosed room, an addition off the kitchen and made entirely from wood, it was our favorite room in the house.

The children, as usual, were full of stories about whatever had happened to them at school that day and were talking, vociferously over each other, to get our attention. Markos was 14 years old at the time and he was half-way through his third year of secondary school. Eva was 13 and she was in the second year at the same school. Diogenis was 11 and he had just started his last year at elementary school whereas Adonis Jr., who was 10 years old, was in his fifth year and Cleopatra, who was eight, was in her third year. They were all busy with their schoolwork and numerous extra afterschool classes in those days. Everyone had a sport activity as well as a musical instrument that they played, and there was a constant stream of traffic going in and out of the house, as each child fulfilled their commitments.

One by one, the children finished their lunch that day and excused themselves to go and get on with their homework. They only had a short time before we had to leave home for their afternoon classes or activities.

For a few moments, when we were finally alone, Adonis and I enjoyed our coffee together and spoke about any family issues; perhaps about the house, or the children, or our family business, I can't recall which. We loved our children, but we treasured those moments when it was just the two of us and we were reminded of the passion that bonded us. When we could think back to the beginning of our relationship and what a relatively simple time it had been compared to the craziness that surrounded us now, with our big family. We both always agreed, though, that we would not change a single thing about our lives, no matter how hard we had to work sometimes, to hold it all together. In fact, I always felt that the glue holding everything together was the strength of our love. Our love was like the eternal flame we had seen on John F. Kennedy's grave, a flame that burnt silently but assuredly, always and forever.

When he had finished his coffee, Adonis stood up and kissed me, saying, "My love, I will go and take a short 'siesta' and then I'll work in the garden; it's time to prune the trees."

Those words sounded so unremarkable out of context, but of course, in time, they became indelibly etched in my memory. I will never forget them! How could I have known these were his very last words.

Shortly after, when I had finished clearing away the dishes from our lunch, I called the children to get into the car; it was almost 3 p.m. and we had to leave to get them all to their afternoon commitments on time. First, I took Diogenis to his English class. Eva had a German class there as well. I dropped them off, and then I took Markos and Cleopatra to a different institute for their English classes. Last, I took Adonis Jr. to his swimming practice and watched him swim for a few minutes, before it was time to pick the first two up again. So, I went to get Diogenis and Eva from their classes, and we stopped at the supermarket for a few groceries before heading home. We arrived home at around 5:20 p.m.

As we pulled into our driveway, we saw smoke coming from behind the low wall at the end of the garden. I explained to the children that their father was probably burning the dead branches of the trees he had been pruning. Diogenis jumped out of the car before I had even switched off the engine. He turned on the tap attached to the garden hose and told me to leave the water running. He thought that his father may needed help with putting out the fire. Eva and I went into the house with the shopping bags and started to prepare the evening meal.

Soon after, I learnt what really happened.

Diogenis had reached the wall at the end of the garden and had pulled himself up on top of it, ready to jump down on the other side, outside our house wall, when he discovered his father lying face down in the dirt, with his body still and his arms outstretched besides him. Diogenis froze and then jumped back into our garden. He raced up to the house calling out for me. Eva, who was nearby, ran to him and asked what was wrong and he said; "I think our Daddy is dead!"

I was standing in the kitchen, with a knife in my hand and an onion lying on the chopping board, when my two children came racing into the kitchen shouting over each other:

"Regina! Regina, come quick! Quickly! Daddy might be dead!"

Before I could even register the words, I felt as if the knife I was holding had been plunged into my chest and was piercing my heart, cutting it in half. I couldn't move. There was a strange silence inside me, and I couldn't feel the ground underneath my feet. I felt as though I was suspended in mid-air. The only word I could think of was the word, "No." I could hear this word coming from somewhere and sounding out, repeatedly; "No! No, no, no, no!" I didn't realise that I was actually screaming the word out loud myself, but instead, I was only aware of hearing it.

I don't remember walking outside, but suddenly, I was out there at the bottom of the garden, where the fire was burning intensively. Suddenly, I was standing over my husband, looking down at him. At this point, he was facing up because, as I later found out, our neighbor, Mike, had heard Diogenis screaming and he came running over to the scene. When he had turned Adonis' body over, he immediately raced over to another neighbor's house to ask for help, as the man who lived there was a doctor, then he had gone to call for an ambulance.

The instant I saw my husband's face, I knew that there was no sign of life in his body, but I refused to believe it. I laid down beside him and tried to pull him up, crying at him:

"Please, darling, wake up, please Adonis, we love you, we need you, don't leave us. Your children need you. Please, don't leave us!" There was nothing. I couldn't accept that he wasn't responding. I started doing mouth-to-mouth resuscitation. Then I pumped his chest, again and again, which caused his lunch to be regurgitated out of his mouth and spray all over me.

Suddenly, I was aware of someone beside me; it was the neighbor who was a doctor. He was gently telling me to stop; there was no more to be done as there was no pulse. I looked at him, but I didn't believe him.

While this was all happening, Diogenis had gone with Mike to see where the ambulance was at in the village. The hospital was only five minutes from our house and yet, after twenty minutes, the ambulance had still not arrived. They could hear the sirens from over the other side of the village, so they ran down to the coffee shop at the bottom of our street waiting for the ambulance to drive past. Finally, it came and they pointed it in the right direction. However, it still made another wrong turn before finally arriving at our house, a good five minutes after Diogenis and Mike had made it back there.

By the time the ambulance staff got to the place where my husband was lying on the ground, I was consumed with anger and was ready to blame them entirely for my husband's condition. I started shouting at them, insisting that they have to rescue my husband, saying that they had to save my children's father. I was hysterical. The only thing one of them said to me was that I should calm down, that everything was okay and not to worry. I was so ready to kill him! I lunged at him and I'm not sure what I would have done if someone hadn't held my arms. I didn't know who I was or what I was doing; I just wanted someone to bring my husband back to life, desperately.

Finally, they put Adonis onto a stretcher and lifted him into the back of the ambulance. I stood in the middle of the street and watched the ambulance drive away. I vividly remember my final sight of the red flashing light as it rounded the corner besides the coffee shop before disappearing from view. He was gone. My husband was gone. Suddenly I felt it all over my body, in my heart and in all my bones. I then knew that he had gone forever.

I had no words. The word "dead" had suddenly disappeared from my vocabulary. I refused to let it in. Diogenis and Eva were staring at me, starved for answers, for some kind of explanation. I felt completely empty. The throbbing pain in my heart was unlike anything I had ever felt. I have never found the words to express how I felt in that moment. The pain that surged through my whole body was overwhelming.

Suddenly, I heard Eva's voice saying:

"Regina, go! Go to the hospital, Daddy needs you!" Her eyes were filled with tears.

I got into the car—our beloved car, the Mercedes that Adonis had bought me in 1992, as a gift for the birth of our fourth son, Adonis Jr. I hoped the car knew how to get to the hospital itself because I felt completely incapable of driving it. Luckily, it seemed to because a few minutes later, without being aware of what I was doing, I had arrived at the hospital safely.

Much later, Diogenis and Eva explained me who had actually picked up their other three siblings from their afternoon classes, while I was trying to rescue my husband. They gladly remembered that their siblings needed to be picked up from their various classes, so they had gone with Audrey, Mike's wife, to pick everyone up. Eva was sitting in the front passenger seat when Markos and Cleopatra got into the back with Diogenis. As they got into the car, they saw that their siblings were crying, and they asked what had happened. Eva tried to say it was nothing, but Diogenis blurted out that their father might be dead. Now, they all started crying and by the time Adonis Jr. got into the car, Audrey must have had a very distressing scene on her hands. She looked after them so well, though. She took them back to her house and Mike put some cartoons on the TV. The children had often been to Mike and Audrey's house to watch videos of English cartoons. They were usually so excited to be invited over to their house, but on this occasion, I imagine the atmosphere was extremely subdued.

At the hospital, I was guided until the room where they had taken my husband and noticed that there was a small crowd of people outside it. Some of his family members were there and a few of his close friends. News had traveled fast. I didn't speak, neither looked at any of them. I couldn't. I had no words. I simply walked into my husband's room. I needed to be alone with him.

As I looked at my husband, lying there, with his eyes closed, I think some divine strength must have kept me conscious; otherwise, I would have fainted. That divine presence calmed me and stayed with me while I stood looking down at my love. I felt as though the two of us were being bathed in a warm and peaceful light. There were no words, just overwhelming emotions.

Several times, the door to the room opened behind me, and then closed quietly again, as if people were looking in, but had realised they should not disturb us.

Finally, I sat down on the bed and put my head on my husband's chest. I kissed him repeatedly and then started to speak to him, gently. As I talked to him, I grew convinced that he could hear me; it was like we were having one of our regular conversations. I told him how much I love him, and that I don't know how I will be able to cope with life without him. I felt in my heart that he answered me, telling me to be brave, saying that he would always love me, that I would be protected, that he would always look after me and our children. My tears ran down my cheeks and onto his chest.

"Goodbye, my love," I said finally. "Please remember, we all love you so much, we need you, the children are waiting for you at home. Go peacefully wherever you need to go and please send us your love, always and forever, from wherever you go."

Finally, I realised that a nurse had quietly come into the room and was standing beside me. She helped me to my feet and told me I should go home and be with my children.

As I left the room, I saw that the crowd of people outside the hospital room had grown. All sorts of people had arrived; most of my husband's family was there—all the women wailing and screaming, as well as many friends and neighbors. I looked at them all and suddenly I realised that my eyes were dry, compared with the floods of tears they were shedding. I had just shared such a peaceful moment with my husband, and the whole crowd waiting for me outside couldn't decipher my composed state of mind. I must have looked like a statue, standing there, still and silent, staring at them all, but I had shed all my tears in that room with my husband and I had no more tears to shear. To some people, I must have seemed like I had no emotions at all, but it didn't matter. I could not talk to anyone; I desperately needed to get home to my children.

By the time I got home, another small crowd was beginning to congregate outside our house. The children were all in the pergola by then, surrounded by well-wishers, who were also offering their condolences to me. I thanked them, but all I wanted was to be alone with my children. I remember, our friendly lady dentist, who always loved the children and was such a kind woman, brought some pizza, but the children didn't want the pizza, they just wanted their Daddy to come home. Every time there was another knock at the door, their little faces lit up, as if they thought it was going to be someone bringing their father home. Every time they saw that it was just another black-clad mourner approaching our doorstep, crying hysterically, the children retreated further into their shells, unable to do anything or talk to anyone. I can't imagine how disturbing the whole scene was for them. We were all desperate for a little privacy and peace so we could be with each other, but people kept arriving.

Finally, people started to leave and when the last of our visitors had gone, I took the children upstairs. We all got into my bed together. They were full of questions about their Daddy, and I knew I only had half the answers, if any really.

"Where is Daddy?" they asked repeatedly.

I had only ever spoken the truth to my children and yet I struggled to know what to say. At that moment, did I know for sure where he was? No. I only had my faith that his spirit lives on and would watch over us. His physical body was lying in the hospital; I knew that for a fact, but his spirit had gone somewhere else.

"Where he has gone... he is happy," I told them, because it was what I believed. "Even though we cannot see him, he can see us and he loves us and wants us to be happy." When they started to cry, I said; "Don't be sad, my angels, Daddy would not want as to be sad. If you are sad, then he will be sad too. He only wants us to be happy. If we are happy, then, he'll also be happy." I told them that I had spoken to him in the hospital and I was certain he had heard everything I had said. I told them that I had assured their beloved Papa—as they used to call him—that we all love him. They never took their little eyes off me as I spoke to them. I felt all the weight of five young souls clinging onto me, begging me to tell them what I couldn't tell them, searching to know, when they would see their father alive and well again.

Through the devastating sadness that night, I still managed to feel a sense of peace. I felt Adonis was with me, right beside me, helping me speak every word I uttered to our heartbroken children.

"There will never be a moment when your father's love is not with you, when he is not watching over you and protecting you," I told them. "We will always light a candle to show him that we are thinking of him, that we want him to be happy wherever he may be."

I wasn't aware of how, nor when, but eventually we must have drifted off to sleep, all of us in that one bed together lying on the fragments of our shattered hearts, unable to bear the thought of a future without the husband and father we loved so dearly.

Innocence. The night that Adonis died marked the end of innocence. Until that time, we were all ignorant of what life could really throw at us. Even I, who had experienced the grief of losing my parents, was completely unprepared for what came next. When I lost my parents, it was extremely sad, but by then, they were not part of my daily life anymore. I had left home, and I was carving my own path in life. Adonis had been ripped from our routine with a brutally abrupt force, and we were completely lost without his physical presence.

I realised, how easy it's to lose your mind when the things you previously considered essential for staying alive are taken away from you. Imagine that you suddenly need to survive without any oxygen necessary or water available to you. Of course, you would die without oxygen, but the pain of losing what we considered essential in life felt almost as debilitating. The pain that now engulfed us was like being suffocated. The need for the touch or the voice of the man who had been besides us one minute and was gone the next, was like an unquenchable thirst that I honestly feared that would drive us insane.

Before our grief set in and we tried to come to terms with life without the beloved of our family, we had to pay our public respects to our wonderful father and husband.

The day of Adonis' funeral was a day that is still remembered in Paphos today. People came from all over Cyprus. He was well-known and dearly loved by friends and business associates alike. At least 1,000 people attended; only a state funeral could have been bigger. My husband's entire family along with all his friends and business associates were there, as well as the members of the political party he belonged to and several high-ranking ministers. Adonis was well-known throughout the island, so it was a huge occasion. Even the then President of Cyprus, Glafcos Clerides, attended, arriving in a helicopter. He and Adonis had been great friends when they were younger. Clerides had helped get Adonis out of jail when he was arrested during the Turkish invasion in 1974. In turn, Adonis had helped Clerides with all his political campaigns. As well, Clerides had become the Godfather of our eldest son Markos. Even now, when people ask about Adonis and his funeral is mentioned, they say; "Ah, the funeral with the helicopter." That's how they remember it!

The children all wore their Scouts uniform to the funeral because their father was so proud of their achievements in the Scouts. They looked so smart and I was proud of the way they managed their emotions throughout the funeral service. I felt a great sense of pride as I stood with them beside my husband's coffin—all of us holding hands and looking out across our beloved father.

Then I did something that seemed to me the most obvious thing to do. I walked up to the microphone and made a short but eloquent speech. I started; "On behalf of myself and my children, I would like to thank you all for coming to pay your respects to a truly great man." As for myself, I am grateful for having had 19 wonderful years, living with the man I loved most and that this love will remain alive forever.

I heard a collective gasp from the crowd and then a wave of wailing and crying broke out (I later found out that a woman would never normally speak at such a large, public occasion, but I was oblivious at the time). I simply continued my speech, a speech that was full of gratitude, and one that called for people to celebrate Adonis' rich and colorful life rather than mourn it. I was extremely composed, compared with the outpouring of grief that came from others. I had experienced grief before, even though it was not welcome to me but it was familiar. Only after the funeral, and for a long time afterwards in fact, did I notice that people looked at me differently, unsure of what to make of a woman who would take a microphone and speak in front of approximately a thousand people. I didn't understand. I would have stood in front of a hundred thousand people, if I had the opportunity to call them to celebrate the life of such a great man that Adonis was.

Adonis was only 59 when he died. There was a ten-year age gap between us so it wasn't unexpected that I would outlive him, but I did expect to be well into my seventies before I survived him, not 49!

I couldn't focus on my own grief initially. In the days and weeks that followed Adonis' death, all I could do was to ensure that all the practical chores got done, that the children had some kind of normal life routine to distract them from the tragedy that had crashed over their lives like a Tsunami wave. They kept asking; "Why?" Why God had taken their father, and not the father of one of their friends, for instance. Why had they been singled out, they wanted to know. Had they done something wrong? They felt punished. I did everything I could to alleviate their pain, but I couldn't give them the one thing they wanted, the one thing they craved for the most. I couldn't give them their father back.

The older children asked many questions, while the younger ones just didn't know how to process the information. For weeks afterwards, my then eight-year-old Cleopatra would write letters to her father, using different colored pens for each word, saying things like; "Please Daddy, come home, we love you and miss you. Please get better and come home." And; "Daddy, I have made you a nice card, Mama will bring it to you. Please tell her not to be sad or we will be sad. Do you want us to be sad or happy, Daddy?" She urged us all to wear bright colors, having been disturbed by seeing everyone wearing black.

What was also desperately sad to witness was Lassie's reaction. She wanted to be close to us all the time. Normally, she never came that close to the house, she was an outdoor dog, but in the weeks after Adonis' death, she would always sit by the front door, with her eyes downturned, her ears limp and her tail between her legs, as if she wanted to say; "Where is Adonis? I don't understand why he doesn't come home anymore."

As if our pain wasn't great enough, I soon discovered, to my horror, that the children were having a hard time at school on account of their father being dead.

According to the traditional Cypriot society, the father is usually the king, the head of the household. There is no family without a man at the head of it. Without a man as the head, a family's standing in society is severely diminished. While my husband and I had no real ties to the traditional Cypriot customs and traditions, our children's friends, it seemed, they were not so open-minded. I couldn't believe that the boys, in particular, were being picked on because they no longer had a father. The fact that Adonis had been a successful businessman, almost made things worse; it was a tremendous hard fall from grace. Much later, I even found out that the boys had become involved in physical fights, which had upset me even further.

Suddenly, I was also aware that I was being treated differently. I found it hard to get any answers to questions relating to our business, even though I had a good business mindset. And on a practical level, I didn't know what I was supposed to do for money. Adonis had always handled all our finances; even our one and only emergency credit card was in his name. Everything had been frozen the day he died: all the bank accounts, credit cards as well as all the business accounts. Diogenis had found £100 (Cypriot pounds) in his father's coat pocket the day he died. That was for the time being, the only cash I had.

My only potential lifeline was the Do-It-Yourself business shop that me and Adonis operated for few years now.

Adonis was a great businessman. His first big business was selling wire fencing, the first such business in the whole of Cyprus. Next, he opened an Adidas shop, selling the branded sporting goods. This was the first shop of its kind in Paphos. After the revolution following the Turkish invasion of 1974, Adonis was one of the first big property developers in Cyprus. He had an impressive résumé by the time I met him. In fact, I sometimes wondered if I had met Cyprus's best entrepreneur! That said, I had never asked him for the exact details about what he owned or how much heritage he had. I had never wanted Adonis or his family to think that I was with him because of his wealth. I never asked him for money or expensive gifts. The only big present he gifted me with was the new Mercedes, after Adonis Jr. was born, which replaced the old Lancia I had driven for more than ten years.

Adonis always liked to be the first to do things; he was a true pioneer. So, when a man had approached him with a proposition in 1993, he was more than happy to hear it. This man was desperate to sell his business because he owed the bank approximately £25,000 (Cyprus pounds). Adonis agreed to pay off the bank loan and in exchange would get to take over the business. The business was a run-down garage used by a couple of carpenters. We decided that I would help Adonis in this new enterprise and that we would turn it into a DIY shop. This, again, would be the first of its kind in Paphos. Until that time, there was nowhere to buy tools or materials for doing home improvements. If you needed a toilet fixing, you called a plumber; if you needed some wood works, you called a carpenter. The plan to open a DIY business where people could buy their own supplies was an inspiring one. However, the only way we would succeed was if I did most of the work because as Adonis was busy with his other businesses. At that time our youngest child, Cleopatra, was only 18 months old. I had to kindly request the nursery to take her early, because they usually only took children from when they turned two years old. She went to nursery from 9 a.m. until 12 p.m. while I was working in the shop. In the evening, when the children were in bed, I went back and worked until I was exhausted and needed to sleep. We worked long hours. It took me many months to build up and to integrate the latest technology available in that business, but it was successful, and so it was worth it!

After Adonis' death, I was more grateful than ever to have the business because it was the only way I could see of making us some money to live on. Although the original account was frozen, since I was a shareholder in the business, a new one in my name was opened, starting from zero, so that I could take payments and pay suppliers. In time, I was able to make some of the money I needed to help with my household expenses. During this time, I also noted that the many so-called friends who had promised their support when they saw me at Adonis' funeral, never actually came through with any help. I felt as though they had forgotten all about us.

I had no idea what the procedures were regarding inheritance in Cyprus. I had flashbacks to the nightmare of trying to sort out all my parents' papers and affairs after they died, so I was grateful when my husband's brothers told me that they would be dealing with all the legal work. I thought their timing was a little inconsiderate—they actually pulled me aside after Adonis' memorial service, only days after he had died, and urged me to sign a stack of forms they pushed in front of me—but I was grateful that they were dealing with these matters. The forms were all in Greek and although I had been studying the language for many years by then, I still found formal, written Greek difficult to decipher, so I signed them all without understanding what they stated. I trusted Adonis' family.

My brothers-in-law were also with me when we were called to the law court a few weeks after Adonis died. Because neither my husband nor I had made a will and the children were still minors, the court had to be involved to ensure they got their rightful share of any inheritance. Consequently, a file on our case was opened. I must admit that, to this day, I had never been to court in my life and I didn't know what to expect. When I arrived, I shook hands with the judge; this prompted some odd looks. I was later told that shaking hands with the judge was absolutely not the thing to do. Another innocent gesture of mine, I thought to myself.

Since there was no will, the court officially had to appoint guarantors for the children. I signed forms that made me a guarantor of the children's affairs. My two brothers-in-law were also made guarantors. I didn't realise at the time that, among the three of us, my name was the last in order of priority.

For the next few months, I lived frugally on whatever I could make in the shop. Eventually, I had to go to Draco, Adonis' older brother, to ask what was happening with the frozen bank accounts. I was desperate to know when I would be able to access some of our money. He asked how much money Adonis used to give me each month to look after the house and children. I mentioned a modest amount. My husband usually gave me more, but I didn't want to appear greedy. My brother-in-law started to bring me this amount of money, in cash, every month.

To be honest, I felt rather humiliated with my brother-in-law controlling our lives. To make matters worse, he started to come, on his own, without his girlfriend to our house every night, just as the children were getting ready for bed. He sat with them in the pergola, our wooden extension, where they were used to having their father's company, and ask them questions, often showering praise on me, complimenting on my strength and skills at running an efficient household. He also praised my ability as a mother which I found rather tactless and inappropriate at that given moment. The children clearly thought so too.

One day, a few months after Adonis died, we were having lunch and Markos suddenly said; "Regina, what's your intention in life? Do you intend to get married again?"

I was so shocked! I couldn't imagine where this question had even come from, but it soon became clear to me what was on their minds when Eva spoke next. She said; "Regina, please tell our uncle not to come to our house anymore. We don't want to see him here in our house. We don't like it." I suddenly sensed their discomfort at the thought that he was trying to replace their father's position in our household.

Like a naïve fool, I repeated her words to Draco. With hindsight, I dread to think what kind of rage this provoked in him. He must have been offended, embarrassed and furious, because it was shortly after this time that he began to punish us for banishing him. I slowly realised that I had a battle on my hands, but at the time, I didn't realise he was holding all the cards.

I reassured the children that I had no intention of marrying again. All I wanted to do was to focus on being their mother. Looking back, although my brother-in-law didn't make any overtly sexual advances towards me, I do wonder if he thought it was his natural right to take the place of his brother—as both the father and husband. Even though he was older than Adonis, he had always been in his younger brother's shadow and I'm certain there was plenty of buried jealousy and resentment hidden there. With Adonis having passed away, I think he saw himself as the new head of the family; maybe he thought that he could simply slip into that role seamlessly. I think that perhaps he must have felt that whatever had belonged to Adonis was rightfully his. I'm sure this was his intention when he started to make these late-night visits. When I think back to him coming to our house, night after night, and the way I slowly began to realise what his intentions might have been, it sends chills down my spine.

As if I hadn't suffered enough, there was even more tragedy in store for me in 2002. My dear brother, who I had always been so close to, called me to say that he was very sick. He had contracted a rare form of food poisoning on a business trip to Russia and he didn't seem to be recovering from it. We had a wonderful and loving conversation on the phone that night, and it was the last time I ever spoke to him because he sadly died in July of that year, only five months after my dear husband died.

That May, I turned 50! I had expected to feel a little different as I turned 50, but I could never have imagined that my life would have changed so dramatically, that it would have become virtually unrecognisable.

I was struggling to cope with everything. I was running the household, dealing with the children and managing the DIY shop. I needed help, but when I asked the children how they would feel about us finding someone to help us in the house, they grew extremely anxious. After the bad experience of having their uncle turning up uninvited all the time, they weren't keen on having a new presence around. I accepted their wishes and explained them that this would mean a lot of hard work for us all.

In November 2002, I received a letter from the district court, telling me that I had to attend a hearing at the law court. There, for the first time, I began to suspect that all was not right because the judge asked why the file was empty! Of course, as far as I was concerned, my brothers-in-law were taking care of everything, so I couldn't understand why nothing had been done. The judge asked me why as the mother of the children, I hadn't entered anything into the file. I didn't know what to say. Finally, he advised me to get a good lawyer to sort it all out. He also told me I had three weeks to return with all the paperwork in order, and then he dismissed me. I walked out of the court leaving my brothers-in-law with the judge. To this day, I have no idea what happened for the remainder of that court case, what questions my brothers-in-law were asked or how they responded, but I was worried enough to call our business accountant, a man who had known my husband for years. This man gave me the number of a respectful lawyer. This man, whom I will call my First Lawyer, asked me to meet him at the courthouse to go over the empty file.

When I arrived, my First Lawyer met me and took me into an office. He had already my file in his hands. He invited me to take a seat and then opened the file. I noticed that in the file there was one single sheet. As he read, he kept glancing up at me with a puzzled look on his face. Finally, he raised his head, looked at me and said; "Why have you appointed me when there is already a lawyer attached to this case?"

I felt completely innocent and told him that I knew nothing of the other lawyer, that I didn't understand any of this. He also informed me that I was virtually powerless according to the legal documents he was looking at because Draco had been entered as the First Guarantor and Adonis' younger brother, Kyriakos, as the Second Guarantor, while I was only the Third Guarantor, a virtually insignificant position.

I was speechless.

My First Lawyer said the only thing to do was to pay off the lawyer instructed by Adonis' brothers and then instruct him to deal with the case. I had no choice and therefore this is exactly what I did. Meanwhile, I managed to get a bank loan in Austria, against the house, the one my parents had bought and that I had paid the mortgage on. With that money, I could pay off the Lawyer that my in-laws had hired in the first place.

From that point onwards, the situation seemed to go from bad to worse. My First Lawyer got extremely suspicious when the brothers refused him access to the bank statements, as well as the title deeds to the tangible assets that my husband and I owned.

Finally, he gained access through the bank and found that the accounts had been drained. There was no more money left in any of them. He soon began to unpick a massive labyrinth of paperwork, most of which made no sense at all. When my lawyer tried to trace the money and title deeds, he was fed with a string of claims from members of Adonis' family that each family member was owed this and another was owed that, and that they had taken what they were owed. We never saw any concrete proof of where exactly where this money had gone, although my children soon commented that their older cousins suddenly all had new cars!

My brothers-in-law seemed to be running rings around my lawyer and there was no end in sight. Meanwhile, before any profit from the DIY business came in, I was basically financially dependent on Draco. He was still doling out my monthly allowance, and not with any enthusiasm. The harder my lawyer worked, trying to unravel the mystery of where all the money had gone, the angrier Draco seemed to get, and the more he made it an ordeal for me to ask for my allowance, which in turn was used to feed my children and ran the household.

It seemed as though my in-laws considered my status as a widow to be the lowest level in society. To add insult to injury, I was also a foreign woman, someone who they had always automatically treated with suspicion.

I had long observed that there was a general mistrust of foreign women amongst some of the locals. Until the 1980s, Cyprus had been a rather quiet, traditional society where women were covered up and kept in the background. All of a sudden, a few years later, the low-cost travel boom started to descended on the island and the beaches became packed with scantily-clad women of all nationalities. In came the Russians and Romanians, the Hungarians and Croatians, the Germans, English and the Swedish, and many other nationalities, to enjoy the good weather and beautiful beaches that Cyprus had to offer. These women were liberated and forthright; a new breed that had never been seen before on the small island of Cyprus. Unfortunately, some of them gave their gender a bad name. There were some who preyed on local men, broke up marriages, split up families, and generally caused plenty of upset. No wonder that my in-laws had their suspicions about me; they probably saw me as a typical foreign woman who was trying to get my hands on my husband's wealth. Perhaps, they thought I would then find myself a new boyfriend and run off, leaving my children with them. Anyone who knows me would laugh at the suggestion I would do this, but that was the point, my in-laws had never taken the time to get to know me. To them, I am sure I was simply a foreign woman who could not be trusted.

Even though I used to act somewhat subordinate in public, playing the traditional role of a wife and mother as expected by my in-laws, by staying in the background behind my husband, this in no way reflected how my husband and I conducted our relationship in private. At home we were equals, and treated each with great respect. My husband always honored my position in the household. But my in-laws didn't seem to understand that. It was as if they couldn't accept that I wanted to carry on by myself and raise the children on my own, even as a widow. When I made it obvious that this was my intention, I could feel their mistrust and suspicion grow.

The traditional Cypriot background that my in-laws came from, more or less, dictated that the wife had no official standing. I had often found evidence of this. For example, when registering at a government office I discovered that they only ask the name and occupation of your father. The mother means nothing, you are only judged on who your father is and what he does. For our children, the legacy of their father was a strong one. He is remembered as a powerful and influential man, with a huge charisma. He is a hero in their eyes, and they all want to follow in his footsteps and become successful as him. To my surprise, I soon found out that many people were judging the children simply as the kids who had no father.

Under the traditions that Adonis' family followed, a woman is always under the control of her husband and under his protection. If she has no husband, her brothers and father are responsible for her. I had no husband, no father, no brother, no Cypriot family, and even not many local friends—more alone than a person can possibly be at just the time when I had lost my one and only true love. From my in-laws' point of view, a woman in this position should either integrate herself completely within her late husband's family, entrusting the raising of her children to his family, or get married again as soon as possible. Neither was an acceptable option for me.

As I faced the endless challenges that befell me, I began to feel like a woman without a husband or any other male relative dictating her choices. This felt like living in a country without any rights whatsoever.

Motherhood. A journey between struggle and prosperity. Indeed, what a challenging but equally wonderful privilege motherhood is. Motherhood isn't a simple role; it's a job with many subdivisions. I now found myself juggling with at least eight different roles to play because, in addition to all my usual roles as being the wife and mother, I was also trying to fill all of my husband's roles. Besides the role of a mother, I now had the role of the father too. I was a teacher, a businesswoman, a psychologist, a nurse, a housekeeper (incorporating cook and gardener) and lastly (but by no means least), a taxi driver! Trying to play the role of the father was hard enough, because it was new to me, and it had to be played alongside my primary role as a mother. It was made even more challenging by the fact that I had a very hard act to follow, as Adonis was a wonderful father to the children, and he hadn't left me with any instructions of how to play his role.

As a mother, my priority was to envelop my children with love and tenderness. Being their mother, I grieved with them and for them, and this was on top of my own grief of my personal loss. My grief was a pain that never left me. Whatever I did, whomever I was with, wherever I went, the pain was there, deep and crippling. Sometimes, I wonder how I kept going, how I got up each day, how I spoke, how I operated. Perhaps, having the children is what saved me at the end of the day. Without them, I'm not sure how I would have found the will to carry on.

By then, I had already gone through bereavement myself, and I was used to this type of pain with the passing away of both of my parents at a young age. However, dealing with the pain of young children was nowhere near to what I had experienced before. The one and only thing that I knew I had to do was to be honest with my children about my feelings, and so, I truly shared my process of dealing with their father's death with them. They always asked if their Daddy could hear them. I believed he could, so that is what I told them. They wanted to tell him how much they love him; they simply wanted to be assured that their father, wherever he was, knew how much they love and miss him. They also craved for his opinion, and they often asked me what I thought their father would have said about some issue. I advised them to go to bed and ask him the question, and the following morning, they would feel his response. They followed my advice, and thankfully, it worked!

In the weeks following their father's passing away, and for a long time afterwards, the children couldn't bear to have me out of their sight. When they weren't at school or in their afternoon classes, they needed to be with me in their every waking moment. I offered them all the comfort I could, and yet, I still felt it was never enough. How could it ever be enough? Their souls had been torn apart; they were confused and sad. They weren't old enough to understand such pain, yet there was nothing I could do to take that pain away. I was powerless against this indescribable grief they were experiencing; the inability to take it away nearly drove me mad.

I will never fully understand how I found the extra strength I needed to carry on. Perhaps, the outside world looked on and saw a regular mother doing what she had to do after the death of her husband, having to raise and comfort five distraught children, but there was nothing regular about our lives from the moment Adonis left us. Everything was a struggle; everything cost us dearly in terms of energy and emotion. We cried, we raged, we slumped, and then, we again had to get up and keep going. During these darkest times of my live, the one and only trust I had was in the power of my countless prayers. I must have been blessed with some kind of divine protection, and infused with a superhuman strength, because that's what it took to keep my family together, as we struggled to survive in our shattered world.

Personally, I didn't just miss Adonis on a general level; I also missed him in a specific way. As well as missing his voice on the phone, I missed doing the things we loved to do together. We loved to dance. I desperately wanted to dance with him one more time. He would find any excuse to dance. Whenever there was music, he would jump up and dance. After his death, whenever I heard music I still instinctively turned around to look for him; my eyes would search for him. Where was he? Where was my husband who loved to dance? Why wasn't he there, dancing? There is music playing; where is he? He loved life, and life loved him. His death left a gaping hole in my world.

The smallest things could momentarily derail me. Whenever the phone rang, I immediately thought it was him. For a second; I would forget what had happened and I instinctively expected it to be him, calling me. Who else would be calling me? We had spoken every day of our lives, several times a day. I couldn't accept that he wasn't simply going to call me one day; it took years before I stopped imagining his voice would come through the speaker when I answered the phone, saying; "Hello, darling, how are you?" I yearned, with every fiber of my body for that phone call, to hear his voice say; "Regina, darling, I wanted to let you know I'm okay. I love you and the children."

Adonis had been the life and soul of the party; he was sociable and popular within the society, loved by so many, and respected throughout the small community that resides on the island of Cyprus. Nothing prepared me for the way our status in society seemed to change following his death. I felt as though everyone treated us differently. As much as I tried to fill the void left in our social circles, and in our family business dealings, I was always aware of how far short I fell from the great presence of my wonderful husband. But the hardest challenge of all was trying to be an additional parent to my children, to make up for their missing father.

As a teacher, I had to teach my children how to cope with their grief, about how it is like being a family without a father, about understanding the mysteries of fate, all that hasn't been taught at school. These new lessons fell on my shoulders, it was my responsibility to teach them, but I didn't have a clue where to start.

We had raised the children to be bilingual from birth, teaching them Greek, which was their father's mother tongue, and German, which was mine. We also spoke English and French at home. While they were able to express themselves perfectly well in all these languages, their dominant language, naturally, was Greek, as this was also the language spoken in their school and community. This had given me an even greater incentive to keep my own knowledge of Greek to a high standard, so that I was able to help them through their schoolwork and communicate with their educators.

The Greek education system is similar to the British one. There are six years at elementary school and then three years at secondary school. After this, students can either do a further three years at the Lyceum (college) or three years at a technical school. The final educational qualification is the Apolytirion (similar to the International Baccalaureate qualification). The final grades listed on the Apolytirion will determine whether a student will be offered a place at a University. Certain courses, such as architecture, medicine or law, require specific grades in various subjects. Many children don't get the grades necessary to study at the University they initially had wanted to, as the requirements are fairly high. Also, at the time when my children were at school, Cyprus didn't have any reputable Universities for their fields of study. Most schoolchildren went to either Greece or the U.K. to continue their studies, which meant they really had to excel since the entry requirements were higher for foreign students. The extra afternoon classes that the children took would prepare them to take their A-levels, in order to get into good Universities in the U.K. I knew this was going to be an uphill struggle as the standard of English education seems to be very high as well (not to mention expensive!). I knew that good A-level grades were prerequisite to be admitted at a good University worldwide.

From the moment our eldest child, Markos, started school, I had, with the support of my husband, the sole responsibility of ensuring that homework was done correctly and that school projects were completed on time. I guided the children at home, discussing subjects with them and supporting them, if they struggled in a particular topic. I communicated with their teachers regularly to learn where their weaknesses lay, and I made sure that I spoke and understood Greek well enough to help them. My ambition was that there should be no difference, in terms of the language level required for helping with schoolwork, between myself and any other Cypriot mother. I also took great care to keep abreast of the details of each subject as the children progressed through their education. I learnt alongside with them, throughout their elementary and secondary school, so that they could come to me if they had any problems. It was important to me that they felt absolutely confident that their mother could help them with their schoolwork. I also saw this as an integral part of bonding with the children throughout their lives. The time we spent studying and looking over problems together was quality time that contributed significantly to our parent-child relationship.

I am so grateful that I had already taken on this role of the teacher, and that the children were used to the structure I had established, and my expectations from them by the time I became a single parent. I dread to think what would have happened if I hadn't been so disciplined on this front from the start of their schooling. I imagine their education might have suffered greatly. But we just kept up our regular routine and none of them suffered any great setbacks at school.

So, my role as a teacher continued as usual. However, when it came to my role as a businesswoman, the path wasn't as smooth, at all. As a foreign businesswoman in the Cypriot world of business, I knew that I would have to master it, especially once I came to understand that my brothers-in-law couldn't be trusted.

Almost everyone in Cyprus had known Adonis because of his political and commercial connections. I knew he had been involved with countless organisations, and as a result, I couldn't imagine how I was going to step into his role, but I knew I had to try. As far as I was concerned, any businesses he had a stake in before he died were now our family businesses and I needed to know what was happening within them. I had no idea how difficult it would be even to start, perhaps because it was clear that my husband's brothers didn't want me to get involved.

As I started attending various business meetings, I discovered that the men involved didn't welcome a woman into their midst. The type of men at these meetings didn't fully respect a woman's voice, unless she was the wife of a highly important (living) individual. As a widow, I couldn't have had a lower status to them. Anything I suggested was ignored, my questions often went unanswered and if I dared to diplomatically criticize a man's opinion he would look at me as if I had punched him square in the jaw.

As I kept on listening, I learned and soon discovered that much of what they talked about in these meetings was complete nonsense, time-wasting discussions that had little to do with the matter in hand. Fortunately, I hadn't only learned to read and write Greek well enough to express myself expertly, but I had also managed to develop a large vocabulary. I had learnt to argue my case in Greek, which became increasingly important.

Greek is a fascinating language and famous for being the language of great narrators and pontificators. The ancient Greeks apparently loved the sound of their own voices, and I have often observed that not much has changed! Greek is renowned as the language in which you could argue a topic forever without ever reaching to a conclusion. The more I listened to these businessmen in their meetings, the more I despaired. There was no substance to half of what they were talking about, much of it was pointless; it all seemed to be more about their egos and status than business. Once I realised, I had to edit out the nonsense, and I had to resolve to listen even more carefully to catch what was actually relevant. They would ramble on as if speaking without punctuation and talking in circles around some insignificant point. To me, it sounded as though they had reasoned that, as long as they just sat there and talked, using big important words and complex sentences, they justified their high positions and large salaries.

To these men, I was a widow, and thus not worth listening to. If they had paid me any attention, they would have discovered that I was a successful businesswoman in my own right, a single parent who had raised and educated five children on her own, who had built up a profitable business with our DIY shop, and no less, a woman who had traveled the world learning from many unique experiences. But they weren't interested. It took a few years before anyone even noticed my presence in some of these meetings, and it was a momentous occasion when they started to do so. Even if they weren't ready to listen to me or to take me seriously, the fact that they acknowledged my presence was already a good start!

In terms of my existing role as a businesswoman, one of the hardest decisions I faced was deciding what to do with the DIY shop. I hardly had the time to run it while I was taking care of my five children, but I couldn't afford to let it go. The shop itself was huge, over 645 square meters of floor space. We had several employees, but my husband and I had always taken care of its management. We had a very loyal customer base.

At first, I tried to employ someone to oversee the business in the afternoons, so that I could be with the children. Twice, I tried to hire a suitable person and both times I felt as if I was being taken advantage of—perhaps because they noticed that there was no man present to protect me. On one occasion, I found out that there were several items missing from my stock list, but no one owned up to taking anything.

Eventually, I realised that I had a choice in my hands. Either I could run the business entirely myself and get someone to look after the children in the afternoons, or I could open the store in the mornings only, so that I could be with my children in the afternoons. I instinctively chose the latter option, and, with hindsight, I knew that this was absolutely the right thing to do.

Given what they had been through, my children needed me; they wouldn't have coped having someone else look after them in the afternoons, and not seeing their mother until the evening.

So, I opened the shop on my own from 9 a.m. until 1:30 p.m., Monday through to Saturday, while the children were at school, and closed it in the afternoons to be with them for lunch and take them to their afternoon classes.

After reducing my trading hours, I am sure many people were convinced the business would fail, but our loyal customers didn't let us down, they were happy to adjust to the new hours and get their shopping done in the mornings. We had an excellent reputation, and that saved our business. Plus, our regular customers knew our situation and understood the reason for the new opening hours. Many of our customers were foreigners living in the area, and they appreciated my ability to communicate with them, thanks to my working knowledge of so many languages. I never lost a single customer, and eventually the earnings from that business helped us survive. Fortunately, I was the only one with access to this business account.

I got the feeling that the idea of a woman, single-handedly running a business (especially a large shop) while at the same time raising a family was unthinkable to my in-laws and many other locals. But I had to do my best for my children; I did what I had to do. I am grateful I had the courage to follow through with my plan, despite popular negative opinion.

Next, although I had studied psychology for two years as part of my University degree, however, nothing could have prepared me for how it would feel to put some of this knowledge into practice, especially with my own children.

One of the worst experiences a person can encounter is to watch people suffering, especially the ones they love the most. It feels devastating to watch children suffer, particularly when they don't fully understand the cause of their pain; it's heart-wrenching. I was terrified that my children's hearts would seal up as a result of the trauma, that they would cease to trust, that they would be too afraid to love deeply again.

Not only did my children have to suffer the private loss of their father, but they also suffered publicly. They became known as the children with no father and a foreign mother, and were discriminated because of this. They were humiliated. I did my best to represent the family in the parents' society of each school, but even these were mostly made up of men. In our local community, it was usually the men who represented their families publicly, even at the schools. So again, although I tried my best, I felt largely ignored at the school meetings. I struggled to understand why I was ignored. Was it because I was a widow? Or was it only because I was a foreigner? Maybe they resented the fact that I wasn't a native Greek speaker, no matter how hard I worked at adopting their language.

Repeatedly, teachers would ask my children; "Who is your father?" These teachers should have been informed about my children's situation, and they should have never put my children through the agony of having to answer that question again and again. Every time, the children had to say; "We don't have a father, our father is dead; we only have a mother," they felt vulnerable and exposed, as if a mother counted for nothing, as if children only needed the protection of their father, as if a mother has no status and no power, and therefore, she cannot offer any protection. The crueler classmates clearly had this opinion and would bully my children, knowing they had no one to stand up for them.

On one particular parents' evening, I went along with my daughter, Eva, to find out from her teachers how she was progressing. I remember speaking to the man who was teaching her Greek Philosophy. He praised her aptitude for the subject, saying she was a hardworking student and obviously highly skilled in foreign languages. I then asked him; "Since she was working so hard and getting excellent marks in all her other subjects, why were you only giving her 15/20 in her essays in Greek Philosophy?" His answer literally broke my heart, and I was glad my daughter was beside me to hear it, so that I didn't have to repeat it to her. He said that if a child has one foreign parent, and was speaking another language other than Greek at home, the highest mark he could give that student was 15/20, that he would only give a higher mark for a student who had two Greek-speaking parents at home. I was astonished! I couldn't believe the level of discrimination and injustice that this teacher openly showed towards a young, gifted girl. He told me that her grade was a perfectly decent mark for what my daughter delivered and that I should be proud of it; but this wasn't the point, he had blatantly told me that he would never score her higher than a 15, simply because she didn't have two Greek-speaking parents at home. Of course, I was proud of my daughter, but I was angry to think that a man with this attitude was teaching her. I could only imagine what other discriminatory remarks my children suffered daily at school. I suspect that they didn't tell me about most of them for fear they would hurt me.

This experience was one of the many key reasons why I decided to send my two younger children to a different secondary school, a private, English-speaking school that followed the British curriculum. I remember, long before my husband had passed away, he mentioned that our children would have more opportunities studying abroad if we would send them to an English private school instead. He was right!

Nothing angered me more than the discovery that my children were victims of discrimination and corruption, especially when it took place at an institution (such as a school) which in turn should have been the pinnacle of righteousness.

Only a month or so after Adonis has passed away, Markos arrived home from school one day, very late. I knew he was due to take the bus home because his class would be running late that day, but he arrived much later than I expected and the rest of us had nearly finished lunch by that time. I immediately felt something serious had happened because he walked into the house with his head hung low, without even saying hello to us, and went straight to his room. He seemed extremely angry. I went to his room and asked him to come and join us for lunch. Without lifting his head, he replied, in a short, sharp tone, that he was not hungry. I asked him what had happened and he said that he had missed the bus so he had to walk all the way home. I could tell this wasn't the whole story, but at least he was communicating with me. Again, I asked him to come and have some lunch; I told him if something had happened to upset him then we would talk about it after lunch and find a solution.

Markos looked up at me, his face full of fury, and then started shoving things off his desk and throwing them. I had never seen him so angry. I simply let him do what he needed to do while I stood and looked on. I instinctively knew it would be wrong to scold him or to try and stop him. Whatever had happened must have upset him tremendously. He was typically a very calm boy, not prone to any kind of dramatic outbursts. I had never seen anything like the behavior I was now witnessing from him, so I knew I had to handle the situation with great diplomacy. When he finally stopped throwing things around his room, I asked him once more to come and eat some lunch with us, assuring him that he would feel better talking about whatever had upset him, after he had a full stomach. He didn't answer me or make a move to leave his room, so I left him and went back to the table to finish my own lunch.

I was extremely tense all through lunch and when the other children had finally finished and gone to their rooms to get on with their homework, I immediately went back to see Markos, determined to get to the bottom of the problem. I sat down beside him on his bed. We sat in silence for a while. I wanted to let him be the first to speak this time. Finally, he looked at me and said, without emotion: "Regina, I have failed my final English exam."

I was totally convinced that I hadn't heard him properly and therefore asked him if he can repeat what he just said. He told me again, quite clearly this time, that he had failed his final English exam. I was utterly astonished. He had always been excellent in the English language. He explained that when he had read through his exam paper, he hardly recognised any of the questions. As a result, he had only scored 7/20. My son had never had such a low score, in any subject, in all his years at school. He was an exceptionally bright boy and particularly good at languages. All the children were excellent at languages. I felt sure there must have been a mistake. I asked if he had questioned his teacher about it. He said he had, and that the teacher had asked him if he had been taking extra English classes outside of school. I should explain, at this point, that in the local school system we had at that time, if you wanted your child to do well in their final exams, you had no choice but to send them to extra afterschool classes. The teachers seemed to absolve themselves of all responsibility for teaching their students to an acceptably high level. This system was grossly unfair as it penalised people who weren't financially capable to send their children to extra afterschool classes.

Markos had told his teacher that he had been going to extra classes. Then the teacher asked for the name of the afternoon English school he was attending. As my son was telling me this story, I suddenly remembered that my son's teacher was related to a woman who ran another English school, a rival establishment to the English school that Markos attended.

My son then told me that he had his exam paper in his school bag because the English teacher had told students that their parents had to sign the papers to justify that they accepted the marks given. The signed-off exam papers had to be returned to the teacher first thing in the morning. If a student returned papers that hadn't been signed by their parents, then the exam paper would be deemed inadmissible and the student would be marked down as having failed to attempt the exam. Growing increasingly baffled by all of this, I asked Markos to show me his exam paper. He took it out of his bag and we looked through it together. I wanted to understand where he had made mistakes in the exercises, so we went through them together, slowly, one by one.

On the front page, there was virtually nothing wrong. There were two insignificant mistakes but that was all. However, when I turned over the page, I saw that it was heavily marked in red pen; the same was true of the third page, and of the fourth and final page. We began going through the questions, with me trying to understand where Markos had made his mistakes. I hoped to be able to show him what the correct answers were. However, as we worked through the paper, I became distracted. I began to get a gut feeling that something was very amiss. I tried to concentrate, but again something felt not right. Eventually, I asked my son to show me his notes from class, the ones that would correspond with these questions. He looked at me, pained, and told me he had no memory of going through these specific exercises in class. I looked back at the exam paper, turning the pages over and over again, and finally I clearly saw, what was not right about it.

The header on the front page of the exam bore the name of Markos' government school. However, the header on pages two, three and four had the name of a different school on it. I was fairly sure it was the English school belonging to the relative of Markos' teacher. After I examined the notes that Markos had taken down in his class, I realised that the exam questions on these pages were of a much higher level than Markos had studied in class. Not only that, but the pages of the official exam paper had been replaced with new pages that were clearly taken from tests set by the English school run by Markos' teacher's relative. Only the first page was from the genuine government exam paper, the rest weren't part of an official English exam at all. Finally, it was all clear to me; the exam had been designed to favor the students who had studied at this teacher's relative English school, presumably to make her school look like the best in town, and in turn, enable her to raise her student numbers and rates. I had never seen anything so corrupt in my life!

I asked my son to show me his notes again, and to try and remember if the teacher had ever gone through similar exercises that had been set on this exam paper. He said he thought he remembered his teacher going through these topics once, orally, but the teacher had never written anything down, or asked the students to make any notes.

With my mind absolutely clear about what had transpired, I told Markos I wasn't going to sign the exam paper. Instead, I was going to accompany him to school in the morning and speak to his teacher. After what we had discovered, he was naturally extremely anxious. He was scared that I was going to create problems and it would jeopardize his chances of ever getting the good grade he so dearly needed in order to get a place at the University of his choice. I told him he had nothing to worry about because I would sort things out. I instinctively knew we were right; his teacher had clearly acted extremely unprofessional.

And so, I did, I went to school with Markos the next day. We went straight to speak to his English teacher, who took me into his office and politely asked what he could help me with. I came straight to the point and told him I was extremely unhappy with my son's exam mark. Next, I pulled out the exam paper, pointed at some of the exercises that had been marked as incorrect and explained that my son didn't appear to have any class notes on these particular topics, and that similar exercises were only introduced to them, a part of a brief oral overview. The teacher seemed to get a little embarrassed and tried to brush off my comments, saying that these topics were easy, and that the children didn't need notes on them. If that was so, I challenged him, why is it that my son, whose English skills are excellent, gets a 7/20? The way he looked at me, I could tell he wasn't backing down, so I decided it was time for me to play my trump card.

I showed him the exam paper, and I pointed to the header on the first page, and then I turned the page and pointed to the header that showed the name of the afternoon English school. I innocently asked him what school this was. His face went bright red as he muttered something about it being his relative's school. Then he said something that made absolutely no sense, about one of the students at that English school, accidently copying these pages, and then him getting them mixed up with the official paper.

I forced myself to stay calm and quietly explained that I wouldn't be signing this exam paper, as it clearly wasn't an official government exam paper. When the teacher started protesting, I firmly told him that I still didn't understand what had happened, and I suggested that he accompanies me to the headmaster's office. The headmaster knew my children and me very well, and I actually had a good relationship with him. I can only assume that this teacher knew about my relationship with the headmaster because my suggestion stopped him in his tracks. He immediately gave up trying to justify what had happened. He apologised and said he had obviously misunderstood me and that he was prepared to give my son a second chance. I insisted that he does the same for all the students in his class who had received low marks, otherwise I would personally go and speak to the headmaster.

I maintained my composure throughout this meeting, but it was a real effort. I could hardly contain my anger at how this teacher had manipulated his students; it made me feel ruthless in my efforts to seek justice for these children. How dare he employ such corrupt methods to service his own agenda at the expense of innocent children! I could only imagine some of Markos' classmates going home the night before, angry, confused and ashamed; perhaps too embarrassed to explain to their parents what had happened. If Markos hadn't spoken out and if I hadn't done something, they would have all believed they had failed their English exam, because they weren't good enough, rather than because they were the pawns in the underhand scheme of their English teacher.

Clearly fearing for the safety of his job, the teacher duly asked the whole class to re-sit the exam, this time giving them the entire official exam paper. Markos received a score of 18/20, which was just as we would have expected. The day he came home and showed me his score, he had a huge smile on his face. He hugged me tightly and thanked me for being brave enough to stand up for what was right. I admitted it hadn't been easy to find the courage to challenge the teacher, but thanks to my actions, a whole class of schoolchildren avoided having their educational futures ruined by a corrupt teacher.

I acted to seek justice, naturally, but I also hoped my actions would send a message to my children and their friends to say that corruption is never right or acceptable, and only by standing up to it and challenging it can we hope to stop those who perpetrate it. I wanted them to know that we must never accept injustice; we must always fight it. Having said that, I confess there were difficult times in my life when I stayed silent, mostly when the corruption in question compromised my situation and I feared for my safety—with hindsight, perhaps I was wrong even in this. However, I couldn't stay silent when my children's rights were jeopardised.

Another thing that I would like to mention is that throughout the years, my children went to German classes, and I also volunteered in offering German classes, every Saturday at the local school in the village where we live, so that anyone could attend them for free. It had been my personal contribution towards the citizens of my village, in benefit of the ones who wanted to learn German, either from the beginning or to improve their conversation skills in the German language.

Needless to say, as much as we try to make things better, there will always be corruption in the world, more than we are even aware of. Throughout history, many who have sought power have used any means available to them, lawful or otherwise, to gain it. Such power-hungry people will not stop short of using corrupt methods to get what they want. If you experience corruption, you must fight it; you must not tolerate it for fear of being compromised further. The battle for human rights goes on, especially in the seemingly highly developed societies. Only with societies that continue to fight for their rights, taking stand against corruption, can we hope to progress.

Being responsible for the well-being of my family came naturally to me, so becoming a nurse to my children in their time of suffering wasn't a new role to me. My herbal medicine training had begun years earlier, in my homeland, thanks to my mother and grandmother passing down their extensive knowledge of medicinal plants to me.

I started helping my mother with her collection of special herbs and medicinal plants from an early age. I recall how we would get up before sunrise and go out in the early hours of the morning; this being the best time to collect most plants. At that time of the day, even in the summer, it was bitterly cold, and often I had to wear gloves while I held open the bags for my mother, as she filled them with her plants.

We climbed up the high mountainous areas, lighting our way with torches, as it was often still dark when we left the house. As we walked, we would witness the whole countryside slowly waking up. First, the birds would begin to sing and then the flowers would open their petals to greet the rising sun. Next, the rabbits would appear, leaping about in the long grass, and finally, we would hear the cowbells as the cattle stood up, stretched their heavy legs and started to graze.

My mother seemed to have recipes for many of the common ailments, as well as many for beauty treatments. People came from far and wide to buy them. I feel incredibly fortunate that she taught me everything she knew. The knowledge she taught me enabled me to continue her work. I even gave talks on the medicinal uses of certain herbs and plants as part of the winter entertainment programs that I organised at the old Paphos Beach Hotel in the 1980s.

When it came to be raising my own children, I very much followed in my mother's footsteps. Just as she had known instinctively what to use to cure my father, my siblings and me from any ailments, I always seemed to know exactly what my children needed when they hurt themselves or felt unwell. We hardly ever visited a doctor. My husband sometimes found my approach a little frustrating because he was a big believer of western medicine. However, I always managed to persuade him to let me try my methods first, arguing that if they didn't work, we could then go to the doctor. Of course, the majority of times my methods worked just fine.

I have rarely been to a doctor in my life, myself. I don't think any of my children have ever even seen me really sick. I know my body inside out, and intuitively, I always know what I need to do when I begin to feel unwell. And when other people describe their symptoms to me, I usually know instinctively what they need. I often feel that the best therapy of all is to simply give people a bit of time and attention. Once people have talked about their problem, they usually feel much better without taking any form of medication for it. Giving people quality time is often the greatest gift you can bestow upon them. I still feel blessed to be able to offer this to my family, friends, neighbours and people that approach me in life.

My grandmother always said there was an herb to cure every type of sickness, and for the most part, I am convinced she was right. The remedies that she and my mother taught me became hugely popular throughout our community in Cyprus. People started to come to me regularly with all their little problems. Often, I discovered that what they really needed was to talk, in order to offload some emotional stress, but they also came for my special herbal remedies. I mixed my own "Bach" remedies for people or made them a special ointment or a unique tea; everyone seemed happy with the remedies they got from me. I never took any money for these, I was simply happy to help to heal them whenever I could. Even my customers in the DIY shop started to seek my counsel; there were times when I wondered if certain regular customers came to buy items from our DIY store simply to get the opportunity to discuss their health and life issues with me!

As a housekeeper, running a household consisting of seven people was a job that I had been accustomed to for several years. However, I had always split all the duties with my husband. We each turned our hands to the entire range of jobs that were required. I was able to do several jobs in the garden while Adonis occasionally cooked. We both had DIY skills, thanks to the fact that we had practical working knowledge of tools, which was also essential for our business. I was also something of an expert in organisation, which was essential in such a busy household.

After Adonis had passed away, I was left with the entire house and garden to run. I really had to ask myself if I could do it all alone. As I explained before, when I suggested we take on help with the household or the garden, the children were against it. The house had become their sanctuary in the weeks and months after their father's death, and they felt protective of their special relationship with the place. They had all become so spiritually attuned to the energy in the house, and they didn't want a stranger's presence disrupting it.

I listened to my children and proudly told them that I would honor their request not to have any outside help on one condition; to equally divide up all the house chores. They all worked hard alongside with me, ensuring that the household functioned well. Of course, I made sure they understood that with their father gone, the duties were going to be more strenuous and time-consuming. They assured me that they understood and were adamant that they could cope, that we would manage together. Sometimes, I think the challenge of keeping the household running helped them in their grieving process, as it gave them an ambitious goal to focus their energies on.

When I tell people that throughout that period of time, when I was raising five children and running a household as a single parent, with not any significant, outside help, they don't believe me. We couldn't have done it if the children hadn't already been used to doing their quota of work from the structure I had maintained since they were very young. Much of our success can be attributed to the fact that Adonis and I had raised them to take responsibility for their home, and the fact that they are all such strong, independent and hard-working individuals.

The children made sacrifices to ensure we kept our household functioning all by ourselves. Their far biggest sacrifice was that they had less time to play with their friends, they had less down time, but it was what they wanted, and I couldn't deny them their request, especially when I saw how happy it made them to keep the family together and well-looked after. On the other hand, my biggest sacrifice was sleep. Looking back, I am sure I had no more than four or five hours of sleep every night for several years. I worked continuously, and at high speed, for 16-18 hours a day. As well as getting practical things done, I was always conscious that the children needed my attention too. I made every effort to ensure I never neglected them. One day, I was sitting with Cleopatra, the youngest girl, at her desk while she was reading a passage from a book. Suddenly, she shook me awake and said; "Regina, you were snoring." I wasn't conscious of nodding off, even though I tried desperately hard not to let it happen, but my children reported that it happened quite often during those years.

As a taxi driver, back in those days, there still weren't any local bus services between Limassol and Paphos that my two younger children could have taken to go to their English private school. So, I had to drive them back and forth five times per week for several years. They still remember one quiet threatening experience that occurred after picking them up from their school, which was a forty-minute drive from where we live. As I was driving around mid-day, the hottest time of the day, on our way back, I often struggled to keep my eyes open while driving, which this forced me to stop several times along the way to take a short brake and to re-energise my body.

For much of that time, I was simply operating like a robot. I remember people would invite me to their house for a coffee and I would think to myself, what a waste of time. I would almost feel offended, as if I was irritated that they thought I had the time to simply just sit and enjoy a coffee. What I now realise when I look back is that I was completely forgetting to live, as Regina. I was focused entirely on just existing. The only time I allowed myself a little necessary reprieve from the daily grind was in the early hours of each morning, when I did my meditation. I am sure I wouldn't have coped if I hadn't kept up with this ritual; it's how I found the strength and balance with which to get through the day. I credit myself with the fact that I never neglected my body, and this, because I was clearly aware that I had to keep it strong and healthy or I would fail to fulfil all my duties. I couldn't afford to get sick. I truly loved and honored my body and I kept myself fit. Also, I continued to ensure that we had an extremely healthy and balanced diet.

Before sunrise every day, I would prepare a three-course menu for lunch; it would all be ready to be warmed up and served within 20 minutes of everybody returning home from work and school. I continued to use all our own food stuff, grown in the garden, ensuring we all ate plenty of salad, with interesting herbs and fresh vegetables added, as well as fruits from our various trees. I used to make my own lemon cordial out of lemons, from the trees in the back garden. Occasionally, I would make a cake for a treat, or buy some ice-cream from the supermarket if I didn't have the time to bake. A healthy lifestyle isn't particularly expensive, and we are a living proof that you don't get sick when you eat natural and nutritious food. You don't even need much quantity when you are eating such nutritious foodstuff. Only when the food has been stripped of its nutrients, as this happens to so many mass-produced, pre-packed items, people don't feel satisfied and always feel hungry. The result is that they keep eating more and more to feel fulfilled.

Meal times continued to be our big family occasions, like these had always been. We all ate together and used this time to discuss family matters, talk about issues that were bothering us, or just laugh and joke over shared stories. These quality times together were essential in keeping us bonded, especially through our hardest times.

We also immersed ourselves in the running of our lives, feeling happy in our ability to grow our own food and manage our property.

We all loved to do work in the garden; planting seeds and watching them grow, observing the animals explore their environment, and generally soaking up all the beautiful sunshine of the island. This kept us focused, energised and happy. We arranged and did as much as we could ourselves. If something broke, we would work as a team to mend it; the children became adept at handiwork. We also had to work seven days a week, with the weekends being when we tended to do the majority of outside/garden work. However, it never felt like work because we enjoyed it so much. We loved being part of a team and ensuring we provided each other with a healthy environment. I am sure all this work helped us heal.

The number and variety of practical skills that the children learnt gave them great preparation for life. They, more or less, learnt everything a person needs in order to survive, as well as exactly what it takes to run a healthy and functioning household for a large family. I remember us all laughing when my eldest son, Markos was complaining about having to do his military service. He said; "But Regina, can you please tell them how hard I work around the house and garden. It's like I've already done my military service, there's nothing more they can teach me." I explained him that things didn't work like that, that I couldn't just get him out of doing his military service. Sure enough, he went and did it, but he came back saying it was just a waste of time, 14 months later! Similarly did Diogenis and Adonis Jr. feel when their time came to go through their military service.

Our work in the house and garden gave us purpose, a happy purpose, which was simply to keep living a good life. I was glad the children were occupied. While they worked hard, it gave me a chance to help them heal their shattered souls. I put everything I had into healing my children during this time.

I attribute our good health to our well-balanced lives. Balance comes from eating well and getting enough exercise, having a good relationship with your fellow family members and colleagues, taking care of yourself in a spiritual sense, and remembering to have fun.

As a healer and life coach, my instinct to help people heal has always come naturally to me. I feel I've always had an intuitive understanding of the human heart and mind, in terms of the complex emotions and thoughts that arise from our life experiences. This only intensified once I had my own children. I always felt strongly connected to them, spiritually and psychologically, reading in their expressions how they were feeling and what they needed. So, you can only imagine what I went through as I witnessed them process their grief.

I have always listened to my strong inner voice, especially when it came to my children. I feel as if I always know instinctively what to do and how to deal with situations as they arise. Of course, the one event I never, in my worst nightmares, imagined dealing with was helping my children cope with the death of their father. I tried to put my own pain to one side while I helped my children deal with theirs; I believed that their needs came first.

After all, I have always strongly believed that something good has to come out of something so sad; it's the natural order of the universe. Look at what happened to me after both my parents suddenly died, and I had to leave Paris. Eventually, I got the dream job that brought me to the great love of my life and the future father of my children.

Indeed, life itself is an unpredictable journey between struggle and prosperity. We simply cannot have joy without pain. Through suffering we learn something new and valuable. Helping my children heal enabled me to grow, spiritually. By helping them through their pain and by trying to explain them how the universe works, I also started to accept the bigger picture; the natural order of things. Explaining to a child that something good will come of their father's death is an almost impossible task, but I knew that if I succeeded in helping them to heal, then that in itself would be something of a miracle. The children looked up to me, their mother, for explanations. Simply by reassuring them that there is a reason for everything, even if we don't fully understand it at the time, I think, I helped them feel secure during an extremely turbulent time.

Adonis Jr. celebrated his 10th birthday two weeks after his father's passing. We tried hard to make it a nice day for him, but in truth, none of us felt like having a party. He had always been the most sensitive of the children, and I think, especially in those early days, he was the most damaged. He completely shut down emotionally after his father died. He was by nature quite a closed character and tended to keep things to himself, but after his father's death, he seemed to have closed himself off completely. Sometimes, I wondered if there was something 'karmic' going on because they shared the same name, as if he felt his father's loss more deeply because of that special connection. There was no local tradition of giving children the same name as their parents. In fact, it was quite unusual. According to the tradition, a child would be given the name of a grandparent, but not of a parent. However, Adonis had insisted that our third son (and fourth child) should be named after him, and he managed to persuade the local priest to baptise him as such. As I observed and felt Adonis Jr. suffer after his father's death, I really started to believe that he felt the loss in a particularly profound way, partly because he was named after his father. He isolated himself from his siblings and was also affected much more acutely on a physical level. The shock and stress of his father's death caused him both digestive and urological issues. I first realised this when I discovered one day that he couldn't hold his urine. I sensed that this had something to do with the problems in his behavior too.

As a result, I contacted a well-known child psychologist and arranged an appointment for Adonis Jr. to see her. I organised my commitments so that I could attend with him. I was filled with hope that she could help us. On our way to the appointment, I explained to Adonis Jr. that the psychologist would ask him a lot of questions. I wanted him to know what to expect; I was trying to calm his fears. I told him that he had to tell the doctor everything; the more he could tell her the more she could help us.

When we arrived, the doctor asked me to come into her office alone to begin with, while Adonis Jr. sat outside playing with some toys that were displayed on the table. The doctor asked me to tell her as much as I could about our background and about the history of my son's problem. I explained everything my son had been through, and everything he was facing at the time. Then, it was Adonis Jr.'s turn. He went into the office and I waited outside. I could hear the doctor asking him questions, but I couldn't hear my son's voice; she kept asking him questions but he wouldn't speak to her. I got worried, so I looked in and saw that he was looking down at the ground; he wouldn't even make any eye contact with her.

After a while, the doctor asked me to come in again and asked my son to leave the room. As I sat down, I realised there was something I hadn't told her earlier. I hadn't mentioned it because I knew it was unconventional, but I was suddenly compelled to tell her about the healing work I was doing on my child.

Early in the morning, long before Adonis Jr. was awake, I started going into his room and sat beside his bed. I would light a small candle and hold my hand a few inches above his base chakra. The word chakra is a Sanskrit word and it means the center where the energy flows through. Of all the seven chakras our physical body has, the base chakra is the lowest center and is located at the same level with the low abdomen. Then, I would focus on my son's ailment, and start to pray, asking the Angels to take care of my child's emotional pain, visualising light and love flowing into his body. I would often notice that my hand would tingle with a prickling sensation. I didn't really know if it was doing any good, but it was my motherly instinct, and I would sit there, beside my sleeping son, for 15 to 20 minutes, every morning. My son never knew I was there, as he was asleep at the time.

I must admit that I was afraid the doctor would laugh at me or tell me I was crazy, but she responded with such warmth and kindness. She looked at me for a long time, without saying a word. Finally, she spoke gently to me. She said that I was clearly the best healer for my son. She told me to continue what I was doing and my son would soon heal; there was nothing she could do that I couldn't do.

"Your children are very lucky to have a mother who can heal them in the way you can, I wish more mothers had this instinct; the planet would be a better place," she said.

At the time, I didn't fully absorb what she had said, I was simply glad she had respected my actions and was hopeful that it would work to heal my son, but as I thought it through over the months that followed, I realised how much power laid within my prayers. If this woman, this complete stranger to me, believed that I could heal my son, then perhaps, I really did have the ability to heal all my other children, myself, and ultimately other people as well. This was a revelation to me; it boosted my spirit. I had been given a wonderful and positive message; I could really heal my family.

I kept up the routine of going into my son's room early in the mornings and continued with my prayer rituals. To my surprise, he slowly, but surely started to heal. His behavior changed; he became more sociable again and started opening up emotionally. His urological problem cleared up too, and he gradually became happier. In less than a year, he was back to his usual self, the boy I had known before his father died.

I intuitively felt that a part of the healing process, for all of us, was to talk about their father every day. Adonis was always a part of our conversation. We never forgot to mention him, talking about what he might have thought about something, or remembering something funny he once said or did. We loved to share our favorite stories about him. Slowly, but surely, the painful image of their father's death was gradually replaced with the happy memories the children had of his best moments in life.

As the months rolled by, we slowly began to heal. But how could we have known that some of our darkest days still laid ahead of us?

Earthly Angel. Even though my children insisted we have no help with the running of the household and childcare, there was one woman who was eventually invited into our lives and became, literally, our earthly angel. Most of the time, I was living in a state of great turmoil, and often wanted to lie down and give up, but this woman was the one shining light, and who kept me going. Her name was Clara.

I had met Clara before, in 1983, when I first came to the island. She was a Hungarian woman, married to a Cypriot man, so I identified with her. Her husband was Adonis' friend and business associate, but Adonis was older than him. Adonis and I saw plenty of them in the early years of our relationship, but once our children were born and Clara's husband died (they had no children of their own), we had somehow lost touch. She had visited us after the birth of each child, bringing beautiful gifts, which was her way, but I had not seen her for several years before Adonis died.

Sometimes, people appear in our lives, seemingly out of nowhere, at the very moment when we are almost at the point of giving up, when we are literally at breaking point. They have the power to lift us up and give us the strength to carry on. They come and pull us out of the dark holes we've been stuck in and point us in the right direction, towards the light. They are like divine beings, sent to fill our troubled lives with love and light. I believe that these people are our earthly Guardian Angels sent to us by the Almighty One.

A few days after Adonis' funeral, I remember thinking that I hadn't seen Clara there. Had she come? Surely, she would have spoken to me personally if she had been there. A few weeks later, she came into the shop and explained that she had been away in Hungary visiting relatives at the time of Adonis' death. As soon as she had heard the news on her return, she had come to see me immediately. We sat down in the office at the back of the shop and I made us some coffee. Then we cried together as I told her all that had happened. I suddenly realised that she was the only person I was comfortable showing my grief to.

She asked me how I was going to cope. She didn't mean how I would cope with my emotions, which were obviously raw at the time, but she meant with the physical practicalities of running the shop and looking after the house and the children. The only thing I remember having told her was that, somehow, I will manage. Up to that point, I had just been getting busy on with whatever had to be done, knowing that if I started thinking about it all, I would have collapsed under the enormity of my responsibilities. The only way I could get everything done was to take it moment-by-moment, focusing only on the next immediate task.

Clara told me to call her if I needed anything. I thanked her and told her it was time for me to close up the shop and go and pick up my children from school.

From that point on, Clara was always there when we needed her. She never pushed herself on us; she never interfered with our family life (as we soon found others tried to do so). She was just there. She never said no, if we needed her. Sometimes she would drop off some small gifts for the children, sometimes a cake she had baked, or a basket of bread. On these occasions, she would just leave the package with a small note and leave, never wanting to intrude uninvited.

She eventually became like a second parent for the children, guiding them and advising them on schoolwork during the few occasions she looked after them when I was called away on a business matter, for example. Even though Clara hadn't had children of her own, her values were identical to mine; the structure and discipline she showed with the children were seamless with mine.

Clara never missed an occasion. She brought small gifts for the children every Christmas and Easter, and on their birthdays. She knew their individual personalities so well that she instinctively knew what to buy them. They always treasured their gifts from her. She really was the only one they trusted, the only one they felt comfortable with, because she respected them, she never assumed to tell them what they should be doing or feeling.

I knew my earthly Guardian Angel was by my side constantly, even when she wasn't physically there. I always felt her presence. She was the closest one I had to a family. With my parents and brother dead and my sister so far away in Austria, Clara was the only one I felt I could lean on. She saw me through the worst times, and she gave me many of the books on grief and death that were comforting me; books such as "Eternal Life" by Hans Kung. She was also by my side through all the terrible court cases I had to endure.

My First Lawyer had been deeply entrenched in the impossible paper trail that he hoped would lead to our rightful heritage for what felt like an eternity. I would hear from him every now and then, but there was always little progress to report. My heart was getting steadily heavier, as I worried that we might never see the tangible assets that were rightfully ours. However, just when I thought things couldn't get worse, another legal minefield erupted.

In October 2003, I received a phone call from a large multinational company. First, they offered their condolences that my husband had passed away, and then they requested a meeting with me. They told me I needed to sign some important documents, giving them the right to develop a piece of land they had been renting from us.

A bell went off in my head when I heard the name of this company. I suddenly remembered my husband giving me a contract (written in English), a few years previously and saying; "Keep this English contract safe somewhere. We might need it sometime." What was unusual about this was that my brothers-in-law usually dealt with all the administration for my husband's businesses.

On this occasion, however, Adonis obviously felt that there was no point in giving them this contract written in English, as neither of them knew the language well.

After the call from the company in question, I took out this contract and saw that it was a basic lease agreement to use the land and run the operation that existed on it. I noticed that both my husband and the company's general manager had signed the contract in 1994. However, from the phone call, I gathered that the company wanted to develop a new operation on the land and for that I assumed they needed my permission.

When the representatives from the company arrived at the meeting, which was also attended by my brother-in-law, Draco, they explained the details of the new operation they wished to build. When I said we would have to draw up a new contract, they suddenly claimed that their plans were already covered in their existing contract. I grew suspicious. Why would they be in my office, if this was true? In any case, I knew that the development they were suggesting was not covered under the contract I was holding. I voiced these issues and the men started to look uncomfortable. Draco was furiously glaring at me, as if I, a woman—a widow no less, had dared to speak up to these men. I politely, but firmly explained that they couldn't go ahead with their plans under the existing contract. Either we had to draw up a new contract or, if they were no longer interested in running the existing operation on the land, they could hand the land back to me and everything would be square.

They insisted that even though it wasn't stated in the copy of the contract I was holding, the copy of the contract they had in their hands did give them the permission to redevelop the land for the new operation. So, why hadn't they brought this copy with them? This made no sense! I asked them to send me this copy. They told me that they couldn't send me their copy of the contract because it was full of confidential information. Intuitively, I felt that they were talking nonsense! And besides, the owner of the land is dead, so therefore the name needs to be changed, I told them. They all left my office with very unhappy moods.

I think they were expecting me to end up as a pushover and to agree with whatever they wanted. Perhaps they assumed that a woman wouldn't understand business matters, and thus wouldn't fight them on anything.

I heard no more from this company for six months, until one day in April 2004, I walked into the office and saw that there were some pages in the fax basket. I picked them up and started reading. I soon realised that this was the copy of the contract the men from the multinational company talked about in the meeting we had six months earlier. As I looked at the last page, my heart skipped a beat. There was my husband's signature. Except that this wasn't my husband's signature, and that I had seen this exact signature somewhere else before, on other official documents.

A few years before Adonis died, I had gone to his office to speak to him about some matter. However, when I arrived, I found the door to his office closed and a real commotion going on inside. So, I waited outside in the corridor, sensing that I shouldn't interrupt. I heard raised voices turn into angry shouting. I wondered what on earth was going on in there. My question was soon answered because the voices suddenly got so loud, and I could make out what they were saying. Basically, my husband was extremely angry with his elderly brother Draco, because he kept signing checks in my husband's name without informing him. Finally, I heard my husband threaten his brother. Adonis told Draco that if he didn't recover the last big check on which he had signed in Adonis' name, then Adonis would take him to court for falsifying his signature.

There was a long silence, after which my husband came out red-faced, looking angrier than I had ever seen him look in all the time I had known him. I decided that it was probably best not to mention what I heard, but it did make sense of something I had witnessed on a previous occasion.

Sometime before this time, I had gone to my brother-in-law's office to look for some paperwork relating to my husband's business. There I found a big A2-size doodle pad on Draco's desk and my attention was caught by something quite strange. The pad was full of examples of my husband's signature. Furthermore, I noticed that examples of Nikos's signature were all over one corner of the pad too.

By the time, I had forgotten all about this, I hadn't mentioned it to my husband, but I had remained curious. But the day I overheard the commotion between my husband and his brother, and realised what my husband was shouting at his brother for, and everything fell into place. Draco had been falsifying Adonis' signature, and my husband had caught him at it. And now, I was absolutely sure it was a falsified signature that I was staring at on the contract from the multinational company.

The greatest irony of all was that I had recently found out that my brother-in-law had, in his possession, the Power of Attorney form that I had signed. Therefore, he basically didn't need to rely on a contract with a forged signature on it, he could have written up any contracts he wanted, in my name, and signed them on my behalf! I had found this information out only weeks before I received the fax contract.

I had gone to a meeting with Draco, Nikos and a local architect. The meeting was to finalise the dissolving of a company that Adonis, Nikos and the architect had formed years previously. There were a few loose ends to tie up and they needed to finalise the paperwork. Assuming he would need my signature on a number of forms, Nikos called to ask me to attend.

When I arrived at the meeting, I discovered that it was already in full swing. Draco and Nikos had started without me, and Draco looked shocked to see me there. I could only assume that Nikos hadn't mentioned I was attending too. All the forms got signed; the company was officially dissolved and we left. On the way out, Nikos took me aside and asked me why I had signed the Power of Attorney form, giving Draco the right to make decisions in my name. I nearly fell over backwards. What was he talking about?

I searched my memory and suddenly realised that it must have been one of the forms my in-laws had handed me to sign in the days just after Adonis had died. At the time when I had been consumed with grief, when I had been so grateful that my in-laws were offering to deal with the inheritance matters, when I had put my trust in them who, it seemed, did not trust me.

Going back to the large multinational company and their faxed contract, I now had a huge problem on my hands. What was I going to do with this contract that, to me, clearly had a forged signature on it?

I knew that the signature wasn't my husband's; I knew it as surely as I would know an imposter's voice or face. I knew my husband's writing. He hadn't signed this contract, definitely not. I could clearly feel it in my gut. As I looked at the final page with the big signature that was supposed to be my husband's, at the missing curve of his letters, at the shaky lines that couldn't have been drawn by his strong hand, I felt a dull ache in the pit of my stomach and my hands began to shake. I was suddenly aware of a cold sweat on my brow and I felt sick to my stomach as I gathered up the sheets of paper and put them into an A4 envelope.

I called Clara to ask if she could pick the children up from school and then I drove straight to my First Lawyer's office. He could tell that I was shaken up and he asked what had happened. I briefly explained the whole story and handed him the faxed contract. I waited while he looked through them carefully. He studied the signature and compared it with the authentic signature of my husband that he had on several other documents. Finally, he nodded, agreeing that the signature didn't look right. With a heavy heart, I said I wanted to take the case to the police. I felt a mixture of utter disappointment that I was going to have to press charges against my own brother-in-law and fear because I knew Draco had many friends in the police department, having worked there himself several years back.

When my lawyer and I arrived at the police station, we were greeted by a young police officer. His English was basic at best, so he didn't understand the contract, which was written in English and other complex legal language. He asked if I could come back the next day so he could take more time to go through it and to get a clear picture of what happened. I agreed and left with my lawyer.

The following day, I again, asked Clara to take over my duties with the children and returned to the police station, where I spent most of the day immersed in the painful and arduous process of filling out a police report. I sat with the young police officer from the day before and went through the English contract with him in meticulous detail. In the end, it took over five hours until we had a full police report labeled as Signature Falsification. The young officer sent this report to the police headquarters in Nicosia for further investigation. I was told that the case would be put before the Police Investigation department and the office of the Attorney General.

While I was waiting for a response, I contacted a lawyer in Austria who was specialised in signature falsification cases; my bank in Austria recommended him to me. I sent him copies of all the documents I had and asked him to advise me as best as he could. There was little he could actually do for me because the case was governed by the Cypriot law and, him as Austrian, he couldn't intervene, but I still found all the information he sent to me extremely useful; I clearly felt it would prepare me for the next step, once my case had been thoroughly investigated.

The weeks rolled by with no word from anyone. Finally, one morning, while I was driving towards Paphos, a call came through from the police headquarters. Someone on the phone told me that the Chief of Police wanted to talk to me. I pulled over to take the call. As I waited to be connected, I heard a few clicking noises on the phone and the reception quality was suddenly reduced. I assumed that the call was being recorded. A few minutes into our call I asked the Chief of Police to switch off the recording device because it was affecting the reception. He sounded embarrassed as he asked me to hold on. When he came back to me the line was clearer, but I could still hear a second voice on the line that made an unpleasant disturbance on the call.

The Police Chief's line of questioning struck me as very strange. He hardly referred to the report at all; he kept asking me why I had opened the case, which seemed a redundant question to me. I kept giving him the blatantly obvious answer: it was because I believed my brother-in-law had acted illegally. Over and over again, the Police Chief kept asking the same question, as if he was pushing me to crack and give a completely different answer, as if he simply ignored my answer. What were my exact reasons for reporting this case, he kept asking? I tried to contain my frustration as I kept repeating my answer, that my exact and only reason for opening the case was the fact that I had evidence to show that my brother-in-law had illegally forged my husband's signature on a critical document that affected my business, and potentially my family's livelihood.

I soon became aware that we were going round and round in circles, and I had the awful, growing suspicion that I wasn't being taken seriously. As the call came to a conclusion, I realised that it had all been about me and not about the case at all. I had a seriously foreboding feeling.

My fears were confirmed a few weeks later when my lawyer received a letter from the office of the Attorney General, saying that they weren't going to pursue my case. The day I had the telephone conversation with them, the only thing they advised me to do was to refer to my lawyer for any further questions. However, later on, my lawyer explained to me that my case had been rejected due to the fact that there wasn't enough evidence available, which would justify the signature's falsification.

I was stunned! I showed my lawyer the information I had received from my Austrian lawyer; it clearly stated that we should expect the police to ask for several original examples of my husband's signature before they made a decision on prosecuting. However, the police had asked me for nothing. I had countless examples of my husband's authentic signature to hand, I could have supplied them with a hundred examples, but they had never asked me to provide these. They simply had a copy of the forged signature and my report, explaining the course of events and everything I had witnessed over the years. What on earth had they based their decision on to drop the case? I really wanted to know.

My realization that the police weren't going to help me with this case was one of my darkest moments. I felt completely alone and helpless, as if I had been thrown into a black hole with no glimmer of light coming from any direction to guide me out of it. What was I supposed to do, if the justice system wouldn't support me? Should I simply walk away quietly and accept this injustice? Who could I turn to? Was I crazy to contemplate fighting my case further, when I had no support from the law? Put yourself in my shoes. What would you have done?

Something inside me wouldn't give up. Maybe, if it had been an injustice inflicted only on myself I would have laid down and given in, but this was primarily an injustice inflicted upon my deceased husband and our children; for their sake, and in honor of my husband's memory, I had to keep fighting for justice. I couldn't live with the thought of anyone getting away with insulting my husband, let alone his very own brother! So, I pursued the case as a private prosecution, with the help of my First Lawyer.

This was the start of an endless legal battle, during which the multinational company stopped paying any rent on the land, complicating the case even further. Interestingly, they never went ahead and developed the new operation they were planning, so clearly, they didn't believe that the contract they sent me was going to stand up in court!

The whole incident left a terribly bitter taste in my mouth, and the relations with my in-laws got steadily worse. I began to feel as though they were trying to take control of everything, as if they wanted me out of the picture entirely, with no family, no money, no property, nothing. I began to believe that they would have been happier if I had packed my bags and left.

The fact that my in-laws had managed to control my late husband's money and our land was bad enough, but when they tried to take over control of our children, this, to me, was like a war declaration.

Shortly after my husband died, when Draco had given me all those forms to sign, he had also taken my husband's identification card in order to get the death certificate processed, so he said. He had also asked me to give him all the children's birth certificates. I assumed he needed the birth certificates to process the children's inheritance claim; I had no reason, at that point, to mistrust him. With everything that was going on, I had completely forgotten all about this until some point in 2005, when Markos was making some University applications. He was sending one over to Austria, to the University of Vienna. He had to include all his school records, copies of his passport and birth certificate. Suddenly I remembered that Draco had the children's birth certificates, so I went to ask him to return them to me. He gave me a sealed envelope, which contained a copy of Markos' birth certificate, and I gave this to Markos, without taking any further notice of it.

A few weeks later, Markos received a letter from the University of Vienna saying that they couldn't process his application because the last name on his birth certificate wasn't identical with the one in his passport. So, I looked at the birth certificate they had returned with his unprocessed application, and I couldn't believe what I was looking at. Markos' last name had been changed on his birth certificate, from our family name to his uncles' family name.

(Just to explain, why my husband and Draco had different last names despite being siblings from the same parents. In Cyprus, two children within the same family can have different last names, depending on what their parents decide to give them at birth. They may decide to name them after the paternal grandfather, by adding an "ou" at the end of the grandfather's name, or after their paternal grandmother by giving them her maiden name. In this way, Adonis and Draco had different surnames. Even though at times, when it suited him to be associated with Adonis, Draco would use his brother's surname!)

I was stunned! Why on earth had my son's surname been changed on his birth certificate? I wanted to know how it was even possible. Surely it wasn't even legal for birth certificates to be changed. I was furious, but I also felt powerless. What was I meant to do? Go to a government office to demand the original? I haven't been to a local government office before. I didn't even know how one would go about approaching an official person about a matter like this. I did not think there was any point in confronting my brother-in-law, and there was certainly no point in taking the matter to the police, after how they had treated me and my son Diogenis the last time. I pictured a scene of them laughing at me, calling me ridiculous, telling me I was imagining things, even calling me a crazy woman.

I grew so fearful. If Draco was able to bribe certain officials, under the table, and get the family name of my eldest child changed to his, what else was he capable of? Maybe he was planning to sign over the title deeds of Adonis' properties to himself so that these would be in his name. The thought of him legally owning our house made me sick with fear. I even began to wonder if he planned to somehow get my citizenship revoked, and get me out of the country, after which he could play the role of the "rich and generous uncle," who was "giving" my children all the land and property (which of course was actually rightfully theirs in the first place!). And did he really think my children would be fooled by such a ludicrous act? It was an insult to their intelligence!

Finally, I realised my only option was to go to the official government office and demand the original certificates to be reproduced. Surely, the law would be on my side when I laid out the facts. I could show them my son's passport, even his Austrian passport, and then there could be no way they could refuse me. I hoped!

When I arrived at the relevant government office, I asked to speak to someone in charge of the official documents. After a short while, an elderly woman approached me and asked me sharply and loudly; "Yes! What do you need?"

I was slightly confused. She spoke as if she knew me. I simply assumed she knew who I was, since my husband had been quite well known in the local community. I began to explain that there had been some mistake made with my son's birth certificate, but I couldn't even finish my sentence before she rudely interrupted me by telling me that my brother-in-law was doing everything in his power to ensure the best for the children. What a strange way to respond, I thought. And then, it dawned on me that she clearly knew exactly what had happened and was already trying to defend my brother-in-law's actions.

I let her finish her tirade, and then I explained her that I wasn't here to talk about my brother-in-law. I just needed my son's correct birth certificate, so he could make his University application because they wouldn't accept it with a different surname on his passport and birth certificate.

The woman muttered something clearly unpleasant about me under her breath, and then turned abruptly to go back to her desk. I followed her and waited, patiently, while she started preparing the certificate. While she was doing this, I calmly asked her that, if my other children's last names had been changed on their birth certificates then I needed new certificates for all of them. I pointed out, very clearly, that all my children were going to keep the name that their father and I had given them, and I made it extremely clear that I wouldn't be leaving without correct and certified birth certificates for all my children. She didn't actually speak to me again, but I watched her throw a few sheets of paper into the wastepaper basket. I assume these were the birth certificates of the other children that had been changed behind our backs. She eventually gave me my son's correct certificate and, after what felt like hours, the correct certificates for the rest of my children.

I left with a huge weight off my shoulders and with all five of my children's birth certificates showing their correct names. From that day onwards, I swore to myself to protect those documents with my life!

Invisible. Until my legal battles had started, I appeared more or less invisible in my local community. Only after my court cases had begun and I started to fight for my rights, did I feel that people began to take notice of me. They started to ask questions, curious to find out how a foreign woman with no husband could possibly defend herself in court; it was something unheard of. The big legal cases were obviously those to do with my children's inheritance and the multinational company, but there were other smaller cases too.

The first case I actually fought and won it started in the summer of 2004. It was against a government department that was illegally using my land for storing large quantities of sand and gravel. In addition, huge concrete pipes were carrying sewage across my land, and workers were parking heavy trucks and storing their machinery on this land. It was a tough battle, but I eventually won it. Not long after this, I found myself in court again. This time it was over an estimate that I had requested for the development of a piece of land we legally owned.

When I first realised that I needed to develop this particular piece of land, I had no idea where to start, so I went to seek for advice from the mayor, in whose village the land belonged to. He was a long-standing family friend and took me to a reliable consultancy firm to get a quote for the work. So far, my experience of Cypriot customs had taught me that when a woman attends a business meeting with a man, the man is expected to speak first, so I let the mayor explain my situation in the first instance; he knew exactly what I wanted, so I had no qualms about this.

This consultant seemed extremely keen in giving me an estimate for the work. Although the consultant (mayor's friend) owned the business, he explained that it would be his son doing the majority of the work on the proposal. They asked me to come back in a couple of weeks to look at their proposals, which I did. Unfortunately, the son had got a little ahead of himself and had assumed that we had made some kind of deal for him to go ahead with the work. When I explained him that all I asked for during the first meeting was an estimate and that I would be getting a second estimate from a competitor before commissioning the work, he grew angry. He said he had already made requests to the land registry office for me. Not going any further, he then presented me with a bill for the work he had done, including a payment for the plans he had drawn up my land. I clearly explained again that I had only requested an estimate from the company; I hadn't given him my permission to make requests from the land registry on my behalf.

However, the son insisted and assured me that I had asked him to go ahead and prepare the work. As our conversation intensified, he started raising his voice, threatening me that if I had changed my mind I would still need to pay him at least a third of the development costs. I didn't feel obliged to pay him anything, but still offered to pay him a few hundred euros for his trouble and as a gesture of goodwill. He didn't accept it and took me to court. We ended up in and out of the court over a period of two years. My friend, the mayor, was extremely embarrassed because this was his friend's son. He had to testify on my behalf as a witness, to say that I hadn't commissioned any work. I had obviously not signed any paperwork, so in the end I won the case.

This case was typical of the way local men seemed to think that, now that I had no husband, I could be taken advantage of. I came up against this attitude several times before as I attempted to deal with some of my suppliers and contractors associated with the DIY business.

When my husband was alive, I had only dealt with the internal administration of the business, whereas Adonis had dealt with our suppliers and contractors, chasing any outstanding payments and getting any paperwork signed. When I came to deal with these matters myself, everything was completely new to me, and during my first couple of months in charge of the whole business, I had some particularly unpleasant encounters.

I had to deal with a whole range of clients, from freelance builders and carpenters to big construction companies. Some of the freelance builders opened accounts, ordered items on credit and only paid up when they got paid themselves. I had very little security, as I was working on trust for much of the time. When I chased pending payments, I was shocked when some of these men asked if they could "pay in kind" (i.e. get intimate with me in lieu of payment). I spent many sleepless nights agonizing over how to get payment out of certain difficult and unreasonable clients. As soon as these rogues paid any outstanding invoices, I never did business with them again. At the other end of the scale, some of the island's hotels were also long-standing customers. They often paid their invoices several months late because they knew that I needed their business and that I would never stop dealing with them.

Sadly, my hardest battle of all was against corruption. I hardly know where to start on this subject; it's staggering to think about how much corruption I have encountered in the years since I was widowed and had to become the head of my family. In my struggle and fight against various injustices, carried out against my children and me, I have uncovered egregious corruption time and time again.

A few years back, for example, I wanted to build a shed on a piece of land we owned, located along the main road leading towards the airport, on which we had planted our orchard of citrus and avocado trees. I wanted a small shed for storing garden tools and other general equipment for the upkeep of the orchard.

I did my research and discovered that I needed to apply for an official license through the architect who had drawn up the plans for this simple shed. My architect submitted the plan to the relevant government department, and I waited for almost a year for a reply. During this time, I began to assume that the application had been lost. I started to investigate this matter myself, only to find out that the application was passed from office to office, until I finally ended up speaking to the head of the department responsible for approving applications. This friendly elderly chief of the department told me that, soon, I would get an answer from them.

Two weeks later, I received a letter refusing me permission to build the shed on the grounds. The reason for that, as the letter stated, was that the road leading to the site must be at least four meters wide (in order to transport the equipment needed for building the shed). I took this letter and went to see the head of the department that I had spoken to earlier. I explained him that the road in question was much wider than four meters; in fact, it was the main road, the one and only leading to the international airport. My land was opposite a large military camp, situated along this road. His letter however, suggested that this wasn't a main road, but clearly, I insisted that there was only one road, because I had driven along it that morning! I assumed that he probably must have consulted old plans from long before the road was built! I said to him that if he needed a detailed plan of the road, I could ask my architect to provide him with one. I also made it clear that I refused their decision, based on the incorrect width of the road they had referenced, and I insisted my case to be investigated further.

Many days went by and I heard nothing. Eventually, I again decided to chase the matter up myself. I went back to the same man. He told me that a technician had been sent to measure the road and that this would take a few more days. Now, I started to get angry. A year of my time had been wasted, just to build a two square meter shed in my garden.

One day, I ended up discussing the matter with a customer in my shop. When I expressed my frustration, she asked me; "How much did you put in the envelope when you had made the initial application?" I didn't understand what she meant. She explained that everyone in the government departments take bribes. If I had wanted to speed up the process, then I should have included an envelope filled with money, along with my original application. I was fuming. I can't stand any form of corruption and injustice, so I sat down and wrote a letter to the Minister of the Interior. I phrased my words to the effect of:

Dear Sir,

Over a year ago, I made an application to the Paphos district office for permission to build a small shed on my land, which is located on the main road heading towards the Paphos International Airport. A year later, I received a letter saying that there is no suitable road leading to the site when there is clearly a road, but your department had only referred to the road plans from long before the road was built. As a result, they refused my permission. Next, I presented my case to the district officer in charge. I explained that the road in question is actually the main road leading towards the Paphos International Airport, and that my land is located directly opposite the National Airforce Army Base. I pointed out that there was clearly a road there, a road that is easily more than four meters wide (the required width for a main road). After he heard my story, the district officer agreed to investigate the whole matter again. But I am still waiting. In the process of questioning how fair this was, I met another local person in a similar position to myself, who was also waiting for a decision on a construction matter. This person explained to me that there is a "tradition" of handing over a money-filled envelope, in order to speed up the procedure.
Sir, I come from a culture where such traditions aren't the practice. We don't pay officials to speed up planning applications in Austria. Therefore, I respectfully ask you to

inform me if this is valid, whether the fastest way to get a decision is to pass along a money-filled envelope to the relevant office, and if it's true, please kindly advise me how much to enclose in this envelope.

I highly appreciate your advice,

Yours faithfully,
Regina...

I sent the letter as a registered post to ensure that it reached the right person. About two weeks later, I received a phone call from a friendly woman who introduced herself as Mrs. Yianoulla. She said she was the personal secretary of the district officer that I had been to see at first hand. She confirmed my identity and then invited me to come and see the district officer at 11 a.m. the next day.

I wanted to make absolutely sure that "no one" could accuse me of misunderstanding the Greek that was spoken, so I asked Diogenis to come along with me as a translator and moreover as a witness. I asked the school's headmaster for a special permission to take him out of class for a couple of hours. We arrived at the office of the district officer at the appointed time, shook hands with him and sat down. The district officer went to his desk, picked up my letter I had sent to the Minister of Interior and showed it to me. Then, he began to speak in a forceful, serious tone, although he seemed extremely embarrassed. He demanded to know where I had got my information from, repeatedly insisting that there was no culture of bribery in his office, and that if anyone is found taking such bribes, then this person would be dismissed immediately. He kept demanding that I tell him who had given me this information. Even though I knew perfectly well who had suggested this, I wasn't going to get this person into trouble on account of my bringing it to the Minister's attention. The district officer went on and on, badgering me, insisting that I tell him who had advised me that bribes would be accepted. I kept assuring him that, honestly, I couldn't remember, and that if I came across them again and it jogged my memory, I would make sure to let them know that bribes weren't taken at this office.

I kept looking at him, innocently, as he got more and more irate. Then, I started to ask him why it took over a year to make a decision about whether a person could build a small shed. He wouldn't answer my question. He was obsessed with finding out who had suggested his department took brides; it became a rather amusing stalemate.

Finally, the officer repeated once more for good measure that his office never took bribes because it was strictly forbidden. Then he showed us out of his office. I was sure that, as unpleasant as the experience had been, it had probably been absolutely necessary. I was right! Two weeks later, I had the permission to build my shed.

As people began to hear about my legal victories and fight against corruption, it seemed that, all of a sudden, I started becoming more visible. People, and especially women, started to approach me and congratulate me. I was repeatedly told how many people admired my courage. I soon discovered that one doesn't need any press in Cyprus; the local community will quickly broadcast any news!

While my legal battles were exhausting, these at least helped to get people to see me in a different light. Gradually, I began to reclaim a little of the position we had as a couple and family when my husband was alive.

Control. Asking Draco not to come to our house anymore, as per the children's request, seemed to make him more desperate than ever to find an even stricter way to control us. My First Lawyer was nowhere closer to getting back the control of our money, so I still had to go to Draco to get the money I needed. This gave my brother-in-law plenty of opportunities to humiliate me.

As well as my monthly allowance to run the household, I had explained to Draco that my husband had always set aside money for some special expenses. For example, Adonis had asked each child, from quite an early age, to choose a musical instrument to learn. Although they started learning on less expensive instruments, they knew that they would get an expensive one as soon as they reached their Grade 8. For example, Eva was studying hard on a small piano because she wanted a real, grand piano eventually. Markos had chosen the guitar, and he had started on a very basic and cheap one.

In 2004, Markos was studying for his Grade 8 when his old guitar broke. He asked me if he could have the new, professional one he had been promised since he had reached Grade 8 and was about to sit for the exam. I went to see Draco to ask him for the money.

My brother-in-law's first response was to ask why a second-hand guitar would not do. I explained that Adonis had set aside money to buy all the children new instruments when they reached their Grade 8 exams. When he asked what a new guitar would cost, I told him it would be around £1,000 (Cyprus Pounds). He insisted that he wanted a detailed explanation from the teacher as to why it would cost this much and asked for the teacher's telephone number. Then, he told me he would think about it. I left feeling angry, upset and humiliated.

A few days later, Draco came into the shop and put something in my bag. He said it was a check for Markos' guitar and then he left. The check was in a sealed envelope; I gave it to my son and told him to ask the teacher to buy the new guitar with the amount written on the check. When the teacher opened the envelope, he found that the check was made out on Markos' name. The bank would obviously not recognise it, as Markos was a minor and didn't not have his own account yet. Why had my brother-in-law done such a nonsensical thing, I wondered?

I went back to Draco and asked him for a new check. This time, he made one out to the teacher's name. He still wouldn't make it out in my name, showing me that he wasn't going to trust me.

Christmas 2004 was one of our worst times. Towards the end of December, I was desperately worried about money. I didn't know how I was going to be able to buy food, or the small presents I wanted to get for the children. I had applied for a second bank loan in Austria, but it hadn't come through yet. The shop was doing well, but cash flow was stagnated, as many clients hadn't paid their bills. As a result, I was paying late on payment of my own invoices. However, I knew I was at least going to get my monthly allowance and I was desperately counting on it. I usually got it right at the end of the month, but as it was Christmas, I went to ask Draco if I could have it a few days early so that I could prepare the food I needed, and buy a few small presents for the children. He said that he would think about it. I waited and waited, but he never got back to me. Finally, I went to see him again and asked what the matter was. He said that there was a problem with the cash flow, and there wasn't enough money in the account to give me my allowance. I didn't understand what he was saying. There should have been plenty of money in the account; it just didn't make sense to me. I was extremely upset. The inheritance matter had still not been resolved, so I was still dependent on Draco to give me this allowance.

In the end, on the 23rd of December, I asked for the money again. This time, my brother-in-law said that he would like to give it to me, but the bank had closed at lunchtime and wouldn't open again until after Christmas. I had no money with which to buy my children any Christmas presents. In a moment of absolute desperation, I called our accountant. I explained the situation and he immediately offered to cash a check for me himself. He said he would bring the money over himself that afternoon, so that I could do some shopping for my children.

When I confessed to my children of what had happened, Diogenis suggested that we empty all the children's piggy banks. Having said so, the children pooled all the money together and there we found £64 (Cyprus Pounds) in total. When our friend, the accountant arrived, I showed him what the children had done. We all sat around the dinner table overwhelmed with emotions.

We had a particularly humble Christmas that year, but we were happy that we had a warm home, some good food to eat, and above all, each other's company. The children didn't ask for anything more.

Another story which moves me to tears whenever I think about it, occurred around the beginning of 2005, and involves my most sensitive child; the youngest son, Adonis Jr. He is the one child who would never ask for anything for himself, which makes the whole story even more heart wrenching.

One morning, I went to Adonis Jr.'s room to wake him up and I saw a pair of white gymnastic shoes sticking out from under his bed. I leaned down and pulled them out; I couldn't believe what I saw. In my hands, I held an old pair of Diogenis' gym shoes, one of which had clearly come apart, but had been repaired with a length of fishing wire. Carefully, I asked Adonis Jr. what had happened and he explained that he had grown out of his own gym shoes but that he had found his brother's old shoes in the dustbin. His brother had thrown them away because the sole had come off from one of them. Adonis Jr. had wrapped a length of clear fishing wire around them to hold the sole onto the shoe, and he had been wearing them for his gymnastics classes. The repair job had been so expertly done that, from a distance, you wouldn't have been able to tell that they had been repaired.

As I pictured my child putting this broken shoe onto his foot, and then carefully wrapping fishing line around and around the shoe, taking care to ensure that it all lined up neatly so as not to be visible, tears of sorrow came down my cheeks. What upset me the most was seeing, before my own eyes, evidence that my child hadn't felt able to come to me for something he so urgently needed, and even worse, I had not noticed he needed it. I still gave the children their pocket money every week, and they never asked me for any more money, but I still wanted to provide them with anything they needed for school. Our general expenses were calculated to the last penny and technically there was no extra money available for new things, but if something essential for their school classes needed replacing, I would always do whatever I could to find the money for it. I knew the children's friends all had fancy shoes with designer labels. I knew it must be hard for them to cope with just ordinary things, and I was so grateful to them for taking our situation in their stride, but I assumed that they would come to me if they needed something urgently.

When I asked Adonis Jr. why he hadn't told me he needed new gym shoes, he said he knew money was tight, and he didn't want to add to my existing troubles by burdening me with his needs. I was so ashamed; I had clearly become so wrapped up in the daily running of the household that my children felt they couldn't come to me, that they perhaps even felt, I didn't have the time to listen to their needs, or the money to provide these.

I was so deeply moved by what Adonis Jr. had done; I embraced him tightly and we both let our emotions come up.

Patiently, I had been waiting for my First Lawyer to make some progress, either on the inheritance case or on the case against the multinational company.

Eventually, I suspected that my First Lawyer was stalling the case against the big corporation for some reason. He kept suggesting that I drop the case. However, this wasn't acceptable to me. I wanted justice. I let him continue investigating the inheritance case, and then I hired a Second Lawyer to battle the multinational company. This new lawyer had been recommended to me as someone who was an expert in signature falsification cases. What I didn't know at the time was that he had once worked for the company I was up against. He asked me to pay an extortionate fee up front, before he agreed to take on my case. I agreed because I believed he was my best hope. By that time, I had secured a loan against my Austrian property, so I could pay him. However, after he met with the director of the company, they came up with a "new" contract. By looking at it closely, it reminded me that it was more or less the same one as my husband had originally agreed to. The company basically wanted the land for another 20 years to develop their new operation, but at the same price they were currently paying (or rather not paying at that point!); this wasn't acceptable to me, as I strongly felt that I needed to negotiate a new rate with them. My Second Lawyer, however, didn't support me in this, and I had the feeling that he cared more about the multinational company than about me.

Finally, my Second Lawyer realised that I wasn't going to be bullied into signing this contract, so he did one good thing; he terminated the contract altogether and made the case a simple one of non-payment of rent—now dating back a couple of years. This was a step forward in one direction, but it meant no one would ever be prosecuted for falsifying my husband's signature.

My Second Lawyer started to negotiate with the corporation, in order to draw up a brand-new contract. He called their representatives to a meeting that I also attended, and we tried to work out the terms. We didn't get very far, and I left convinced that my Second Lawyer was more interested in helping the other side instead of me. Indeed, the following day he wrote to me explaining that, since he hadn't been successful in getting both parties to agree to terms and consequently, he was going to resign from the case. I was disappointed, of course, but nothing prepared me for the next blow.

I had initially paid this lawyer a fee of €4,000 (Cyprus had joined the European Union by this time) to cover the work he was going to do in contract negotiations (despite the fact that he never made any progress in the original matter—the signature falsification case). This fee covered our initial meeting and the work he had done. I went to see him one more time in his office, to ask him to go back to the company and see if he could negotiate a new contract (the result of which was his letter to say that no agreement could be made and that he was resigning). For this second meeting and all the necessary negotiations, he sent me an invoice for €15,000!

I couldn't even bring myself to answer this letter, let alone pay the extortionate €15,000 invoice. I shoved both the letter as well as the invoice into the back of a drawer in my desk and left them there, while I started to investigate the legislation about legal fees. I asked the court for a schedule of fees that a lawyer can reasonably charge for a case such as mine.

The Second Lawyer was seemingly in a hurry to get his money, and as I didn't reply to his letter either, he finally took me to court for not paying his fees. That day of the court case, I presented the official schedule of fees I had obtained from the court to show that he had tried to charge me far more of what was acceptable for the nature of the work. I offered to pay an appropriate fee within the range set out in the official schedule of fees, and no more. Finally, I won the case. His only response was to say, pompously, that he had never been asked to justify his fees before. I then looked him straight in the eyes, and all I could say at that moment was that he would never again be able to make such a statement!

I never heard from him again.

However, I was left in limbo again, with nobody representing my case against the multinational company. The police had refused to pursue the criminal case against my brother-in-law. My

Second Lawyer had cancelled the original contract, suggesting we just go for suing them for not paying the rent, as well as not drawing up a new contract, but had then dropped the case when he couldn't negotiate with the new terms.

Having promised to myself that I wouldn't be beaten, I started to look for a Third Lawyer. When I found one (who happened to be a woman), she immediately understood my predicament; she was extremely compassionate and sympathetic when she realised how badly I had been treated up to this point. She said she was sure she could help me. I had an immense feeling of relief and safety, as I explained every detail of my story to this sharp and logical woman.

So, we started from scratch and went back to the drawing board. Of course, it wasn't a smooth sailing. My First Lawyer refused to cooperate with my Third Lawyer unless I paid him a fee of around €4,000. I had no choice but to comply. My Third Lawyer went back and forth with the company, trying to get an agreement with them. She soon discovered how arrogant they were; they assumed they had the upper hand and that they could have whatever they wanted. I still had the feeling that they thought they could beat me, because I was a single woman without a husband. For this reason, I was particularly glad that it was a woman going in to fight for me now!

Meanwhile, at long last, my First Lawyer had a breakthrough in the inheritance case. He managed to prove that Adonis' brothers weren't acting correctly as guarantors for the children. He somehow managed to get me from this point onwards officially entered as the first guarantor, together with himself as the second guarantor. Finally, we were getting somewhere! The first thing we discovered, however, was that there was no money left at all. My husband's brothers had drained the accounts. Every penny of liquid asset was gone!

Fortunately, they hadn't sold our land. With my new status, as first guarantor, I became the custodian of the title deeds to the land, and I put a large piece of real estate on the market.

I was aware that the next ten years would cost me a fortune in supporting all my children through University. I also needed to clear off the debts I had incurred in Austria, by taking emergency loans against my property there.

When they realised that they were losing control over the heritage case, because all the title deeds came back to me, to the rightful owner (ironically forgetting that they still had my signed Power of Attorney form and could, technically, have used that to usurp me) then some of my in-laws started to turn really nasty towards us. In the summer of 2005, everything came to a heat.

Perhaps, in frustration over losing control of us when he was demoted as first guarantor, Draco seemed desperate to find other ways to infiltrate our lives. On several occasions, I intentionally walked into the office from the back of the shop, only to find him there, looking at paperwork. Once, I even found him searching my personal belongings. His behavior had often been very odd, but when it started to frighten my children, it pushed me to a break point.

While I was working in the shop one particular Saturday morning, the children were all at home doing their duties around the house and in the garden. My brother-in-law suddenly entered the shop, and, without a word, he went to where I always left my handbag, opened it, took my car keys and left. This all happened in a matter of seconds. I hardly had time to register his presence.

I only got to the front door of the shop in time to see the back of my car disappearing up the road. I was completely baffled, but I had a shop full of customers to serve and I had no time to deal with the strange behavior of my brother-in-law. I was completely stunned to see him back again after a fairly short time. Again, he walked in without acknowledging me, put the keys back in my bag and walked out of the shop. As I said, the shop was particularly busy that Saturday morning, so I wasn't able to confront him.

About half an hour later, the phone rang. I went into the back office and picked it up; it was my daughter, Cleopatra. She said my name in such a nervous, shaky voice, and I was immediately alarmed. I thought something bad might have happened. I tried to stay calm myself as I asked her; "What, sweetheart? What is it?"

"Regina, can you hear me?" Cleopatra continued, clearly struggling to talk. I urged her to continue, reassuring her that everything was okay, that I could hear her. Finally, it all came gushing out; "Regina," she whispered, "Our uncle came, he was here. He asked us where you were and we said you were at work. Then he went through all the rooms in the house. I followed him and I stood in the doorways watching him open all the cupboards. He went into your bedroom, Mummy, and opened the wardrobes and your drawers with your underwear and then he looked under the bed. I asked him what he was looking for, but he wouldn't answer me, he just asked me where my siblings were. I told him they were outside working in the garden. And then he left. Please come home, Regina, I'm so frightened. I'm scared he'll come back again!"

I was numb with anger and fear. I had to keep my voice calm to reassure my little girl, but I was shaking from head to toe as I told her I would be there as soon as I could, and that she shouldn't worry, that she should go find her siblings and stay close by them until I got there. I assured her that I would be there very soon, and that I would make sure their uncle would never return.

As I put down the phone, I realised that I couldn't move my feet; I was paralysed from shock. I cannot describe the emotions I felt at that point. If you have children and have ever witnessed someone seriously frightening them for no apparent reason, you will understand how furious I felt.

For the first time, I had spoken aloud to myself, saying that "I will not be a victim any longer." "Finish, enough is enough," I shouted out loud, even though I was alone in the office. I had suffered enough; my children had suffered enough! He had gone one step too far. He had held a red flag up to a bull (literally; my astrological sign is Taurus!). I was engulfed with rage. In fact, I was so angry that I actually plunged my fist into my glass-topped desk and shattered it. My employees rushed into the office when they heard the sound of breaking glass. They were shocked to see the state I was in and asked me what they could do. I told them, in quite a controlled voice, that there was nothing they could do. Only I could fix this situation, and I was determined to make it happen. No matter what will happen to us, I was determined that I wouldn't accept this behavior from my brother-in-law any longer.

I asked my employees to leave my office, apologising for alarming them, and then I picked up the phone and dialed my brother-in-law's number. I calmly asked him to come into my office immediately because I wanted to talk to him. Actually, I wanted to do more than just talk to him, I wanted to make him suffer for what he had put us through, but I knew I would have to control myself; I certainly didn't want to sink to his level!

I think my calm, but icy tone of voice over the phone must have frightened him because he was there within minutes; he must have been literally around the corner from the shop, as he was there so fast. His head was bent towards the ground, as he stood in the doorway and it was awhile before he looked at me. The way my eyes bored into him with fury, I am surprised they didn't burn a hole right through his head. I asked him to come right into the office and close the door. It was an effort to control my voice, but I didn't want to shout. I wanted him to know that I was calm but ruthless, that I meant serious business. My whole body was shaking, but I focused on keeping my voice steady. He looked anywhere but directly into my eyes; this was a good thing because they were so full of fire, they would have burned his own eyes out, had he looked directly at me.

"Who gave you the permission to enter my house and look through my drawers and wardrobes?" I asked him. He didn't answer; he just kept staring at a spot on the opposite wall. "You listen to me," I said to him. "You have gone too far and you will not go a step further. Do you understand? I forbid you to come to my house! I forbid you to disturb my children ever again! Is that clear?"

What came out of his mouth next was like an evil, dark twisted voice. With the amount of poison that flowed out of that man,

I'm surprised I've lived to tell the tale. It was as if some dark, venomous force had been unleashed in him. He approached me, spitting at me, and screaming in Greek, "You whore," he yelled, and spat at me again. "You're a whore! You killed my brother! You are a whore!" I felt the poisonous energy of his words hit me, physically, before I even heard them. I never, ever want to experience this terrible feeling again; it was like being covered in thick, black slime. The negative vibrations that were engulfing me were so thick and powerful they overwhelmed me. I felt as though I was drunk, as though I was going to lose consciousness. It was like someone had just poured a container full of stinking sewage over my head.

Somehow, I got past the wild monster that was standing in my office and opened the door to my office. I stared at him, pointed my finger at him and said; "Out! Get out! Get out of my office, now!" I think I actually pushed him out. Disgusting words still poured out of his mouth as I pushed him out. Thankfully, I didn't even understand half of them, as these were in garbled Greek. When I finally pushed him out of the front door of the store, I stumbled back into my office and collapsed in my chair. My employees came in, staring at me, completely stunned. One of the girls asked me what I needed, if she should get me some water. I asked them to call the police. They didn't move. I snapped—the fear and anger overwhelming me—and shouted; "Call the police!"

They all edged out of my office and whether they actually called the police or not, I will never know. I was certainly never aware if they had contacted the police department. I am sure they were frightened of my brother-in-law and with him being a local man and me being a foreign woman, they probably didn't want to get involved.

I sat in my office chair trying to control my breathing. Finally, I felt a calm descend upon me, like the moments after an earthquake, when the earth comes to rest, shaken and bruised, but over the assault. I swore I would never let that man harm me again. I knew that I would fight until my last drop of blood to keep him away from me and to protect my children from his madness. It was the last time I would ever let him disturb our peace. I made a solemn promise to do whatever it took to ensure he couldn't get near us, ever again.

I was just recovering my senses; when I heard the phone ring. I picked it up and it was Diogenis. He was demanding that I come home and take him to the police station because he wanted to report his uncle. He explained that his uncle had called the house phone moments ago and had shouted down the telephone; "Listen to me! Your mother wants to destroy you! She wants to kill you! Believe me, I am your uncle and I can tell you that she wants to kill you!"

Diogenis replied to his uncle; "If you ever call us again, I will hang up and immediately call the police!" Diogenis was furious. He was then only 14 years old. He kept yelling at me to come home, so I could take him to the police station to make a report about his uncle. He then hung up on me. I cradled the phone in my hands; all I could think was, please, please let this end. I closed up the shop, letting my employees go home early, and drove home.

When I arrived home, the children were all sitting outside on a bench under a tree. They were waiting for me to explain what had happened. I couldn't contain my emotions. I started crying and saying over and over again that I love them, that they must not believe what their uncle had said over the phone. I told them that he was probably sick in the head and didn't understand what he was doing.

"Do you really think I want to destroy you? You are my flesh and blood!" I kept saying. Cleopatra got really frightened and started pleading with me to stop crying. All the children then started telling me that they love me and despised their uncle. They said they needed me, that there was no ill feeling in them towards me. They said they would be lost without me, that they only wanted me to be well. I wouldn't be surprised if they suspected that I was losing my mind the way I was sobbing; I was exhausted.

Then, Diogenis reminded me that we should go to the police station, as he insisted to report his uncle. He told me that he had already called to make a report and the police officer was waiting for him. I couldn't have refused him. He also insisted that he wanted to speak to the policeman, without me interfering and that I had to promise him not to do so.

When we arrived at the police station, Diogenis jumped out of the car, without waiting for me, and ran inside. I parked the car and joined him inside where I saw that an elderly police officer was indeed waiting for us. My heart sank, as if I had known it from the beginning that the local police were all friends of Draco. I already understood where this was heading, but I had to let my son go through with his intention to prosecute his uncle, there was no talking him out of it.

Diogenis sat down in front of the police officer and started his story. I noticed that the officer wasn't taking any notes and even worse, had half an eye on the TV screen on the wall. Eventually he asked Diogenis the name of this terrible uncle who had threatened his siblings and their mother. When Diogenis stated his uncle's name, of course the officer said he knew Draco well, stating that Draco was a member of the community, and that it wasn't possible he had behaved in the way Diogenis had described. Adding to this, he scolded my son, saying he should be ashamed of trying to report his uncle and telling lies, and told him to go home and calm down. At this point, I turned red and became furious for a second time, telling him that his job hasn't been done correctly.

After that, I realised that all was lost, that we had no hope of justice; we drove home, both of us in tears. I am sure this moment triggered my son's decision, later in life, to study criminal investigation. He never forgot how enraged he felt at having been disbelieved and dismissed by that police officer; it left him raging over the fact that the legal system we live with was so corrupt and unjust.

For a few days, I couldn't get one particular question out of my head. Even though he was hysterical and was spouting toxic nonsense, what had actually prompted my brother-in-law to call me a "whore" and accuse me of "killing his brother?" Was this what he really thought? The question burned in my mind for several nights, before suddenly and clearly, I had the answer; it all related to a huge incident that had blown up a year or so before my husband's passing. From this moment, I started to form a theory for what laid behind everything that had been going on.

Jealousy. There is nothing more damaging in this world than the curse of jealousy. I experienced the outcome of intense jealousy once in my life, when a school friend in Austria viciously spread false rumors about me because she was jealous of my friendship with another girl. I will never forget how vicious she got, all fueled by her jealousy.

Now, I wondered if Draco had become infected with acute jealousy of his brother. Maybe he envied his brother's skills, his businesses, his brother's hard-earned fortune, his wife, and even his children. If so, no wonder he had behaved in a way that seemed to be aimed at destroying his only immediate family. As I began to think in those terms, I remembered an incident, a long drama in fact, that had taken place about a year before Adonis passing. Suddenly, I wondered if that episode had also been fueled by Draco's jealousy, even though at the time, I had believed that the original perpetrator was a woman who had come to work for us.

I was very proud of the DIY business that my husband and I had built overtime. From the beginning, it had been my ambition to create an automated scanning system. If I succeeded, we would be the first business on the island to have such an automated computerised system. The advantage of installing this system would allow us to offer a unique (at that time in Cyprus) service like the ability for our customers to pre-order special items, for example a particular paint color that we didn't stock. They could pay us in advance and we would then order the items for them. The work involved in creating such system was long and laborious. We had over 14,000 items in our inventory, and I had to create an electronic profile for each item. At the time, computers were nothing like they are today. Every single detail about each item, like the supplier's name, the sales representative's name, the item's code, the cost price, the selling price, the quantity we should keep in stock, and the stock level that would trigger a re-order had to be manually logged into each profile in order to create a unique bar code that would hold all the relevant information for each specific item. This project took me over three years to complete.

This "modern" system I proposed, however didn't sit well with my brother-in-law, whose idea of an efficient system was to sit at a table near the door, taking the customer's money and making a note, by hand, of every item sold. This was the only way he thought it was possible to keep a check of the stock. Looking back, he was probably worried for his future. Once my automated system was in place, he would be out of a job. I guess he must have resented my ambitious ideas; he was very old-fashioned and I jarred against his desire to do things in a traditional way. But I was undeterred; I was very excited about the prospect of this new system. I even took up lessons to help me learn all the computer skills I needed. I trained all our employees, and even my husband learnt the system, coming into the shop from 7:00 until 9:00 a.m. every day for a period of time, in order to learn the necessary skills required to operate this new system.

We were always looking for trustworthy and serious employees, so, in early 1999, when Bianca walked into the shop looking for a job, having just arrived in Cyprus from Romania, we took her on. She impressed us and worked hard, always being friendly with customers and coming up with new ideas that might improve the business.

I got on extremely well with Bianca, and I thought my husband did too, so I was surprised one day when Adonis came home and said that he didn't want Bianca to work for us any longer. I was literally shocked! I asked him for some kind of explanation. He didn't spell it out for me, but he sensed that Bianca had been getting too friendly with him, perhaps even being a little flirtatious, and it made him feel uncomfortable. First, I was sad to lose a hard-working employee, but obviously, I had to support my husband's wish. I asked him if he was going to speak to her or if he wanted me to do it. He said he would prefer if I was the one who spoke to her.

The next day, I called Bianca into my office and I said to her that I was very sorry that we couldn't afford to keep her on, as the business hadn't been great and we were planning to reduce our staff. She didn't seem too upset but asked me if she could work for two more weeks while she looked for another job. I agreed.

I don't know what happened during those two weeks, if Bianca was secretly extremely angry with me, or if my husband was angry that she was still there, but there was a terrible atmosphere in the shop. Bianca would suggest ideas to me, privately, but when I shared her ideas with my husband, in front of her, she denied having ever spoken to me about them, and suggested I was lying for some reason. Her behavior was very strange and inconsistent, and I was actually relieved when she left. She had found employment with a couple who ran a business down the street, and I looked forward to the end of the bad atmosphere she had created between me and my husband. However, this bad atmosphere between Adonis and me only got worse. He was always snapping at me; he had never spoken sharply to me in his life. He also seemed really miserable all the time, and I think even the children noticed something was different about their father. He was beginning to look unhealthy and ill. I grew worried about him, but he wouldn't open up.

Finally, one Saturday, when we were all in the car on the way to a wedding, we found out the reason for his terrible mood swing. We started with a discussion about the shop, when he suddenly started shouting at me, accusing me of having a "boyfriend." I had never heard such nonsense in my life; it completely sideswiped me.

Gradually, it emerged that Bianca and Draco had told Adonis that I was having an affair with someone, and that I was doing it when I was working late in the shop at night working on the automated system. But that was not all. Apparently, Draco had also told my husband that he had seen me taking money out of the cash register. I was furious. I started yelling and crying, telling him that what they were suggesting was ridiculous. By the time we got to the wedding, the children were all crying too. In the end, only Diogenis went inside with his father in order to congratulate the newlyweds and give them our wedding gift. I stayed in the car with the other children. I was too upset to socialise.

On the way home, I told Adonis in a quiet and composed way; "Listen, if you can find this 'boyfriend' you accuse me of having, I will pack my bags and leave. I will leave with what I came with. I will leave my children and go back to Austria." That really shut him up. He knew, I would never threaten to leave my children if there was any chance I had been proved wrong. He had to believe me.

However, it seemed he still needed a proof.

One night, a few weeks later, he came down to the shop and surprised me while I was working. This was clearly his attempt to catch me out. Shortly before midnight, he entered the shop silently, and when he crept into the office, I nearly jumped out of my skin. Of course, all he found was me, sitting at my desk, alone, working.

From this moment on, Adonis knew everyone had been lying and spreading false rumors about me. He was furious with his brother; the incident drove a massive stake between them, one that hadn't been resolved until his time of passing. After the incident in the shop, with Draco spouting all those terrible accusations at me, calling me a "whore" and accusing me of killing his brother, I went back over the bad post-Bianca period in my head and I realised that, although Adonis and I had moved on from this incident, he had never made peace with his brother. Perhaps, this had been torturing Draco and making him behave in such an awful way towards me. Maybe, it was a subconscious guilt that had translated into hatred towards me.

Adonis never apologised to me directly after he realised he had falsely accused me, but he did get angry with himself, saying;

"Why didn't I listen to you, my wife? Why did I let these people convince me of something that wasn't true?" The incident really distanced Adonis from his entire family; maybe his siblings blamed me for this because they couldn't blame their brother, especially not their deceased brother.

As I trawled my memories, I also started to think about the results of my husband's autopsy. The official cause of Adonis' death was a burst aneurysm (which is like a blood-filled balloon in the wall of a blood vessel) in his heart. However, they also discovered that about a third of his heart was already dead before his passing. He had suffered a minor heart attack before without him having been aware of. Now, I began to wonder if the stress of this horrible episode had contributed to his death. With sad irony, I realised that I would have had far more reason to shout back at my brother-in-law; "Actually you are the one who killed him!" But I would never have considered doing that, no matter how angry I felt.

Once Adonis and I got over the aforementioned unpleasant rocky patch, we resumed our happy union; in fact, a weight seemed to lift off our entire family, and my husband and I became more passionate than ever. I even remember a little romantic moment between us the morning of the day he died. I was working at my desk in the shop and he came in to see me and to show me something. He held in his hand a plate of small pickled birds—a traditional Cypriot delicacy called "ambelopoulia." These tiny songbirds are trapped using sticks covered with glue. Because they are so small; the process of removing the entrails of the birds is considered not to be cost effective, so the birds are pickled and then can be swallowed whole. Not very appealing really, as I told my husband when he held out the plate to me. He reminded me that they were considered as an "aphrodisiac." I teased him by asking him if he needed a "Viagra." He kissed me and said; "Darling, you are my Viagra!"

Literally, we had spent 19 years together, 13 of them married, and apart from that one unpleasant period that had been constructed by people, we never lost the passion, that intense attraction that kept us together. We were a happy couple, deeply in love, from the moment we met until the day the Creator had taken him back home. Today, while writing these words, I have come to the awareness that, as I have witnessed that feeling of love myself, "genius" love never ends. That powerful vibration has kept me alive and had given me the strength to move forward.

With Draco out of our lives, we got on with what became a hectic time for all of us. Markos had just been called up to do his national service that all secondary school graduates have to do, Eva was in her final year at school, studying for her Apolytirion, with Diogenis two years behind her, and the younger two had started at their new English private school in Limassol.

The English school was 70 kilometers from home, down the coast to the East, and at that time there were no buses between Paphos and Limassol. I am sure many parents will identify with me when I say I often felt like a "taxi driver" during that time; every family with multiple children knows what a constant crazy juggling act it is, trying to get all the children to their various engagements, and then back home again. Now, I was spending more time in the car than ever before. With the two round trips to the English school per day, plus driving around Paphos, dropping kids off and picking them up from their afternoon lessons and activities, I could easily clock up around 300 kilometers per day. I am sure some professional taxi drivers don't drive that much every day! I spent so much time in the car that I sometimes felt as if it was an extension of my own body.

The car, the one my husband had bought me after the birth of Adonis Jr., was particularly special to me, to all of us, in fact. It was a brand-new Mercedes Model 124 saloon. At the time, there were only four of them on the island, and I felt extremely proud of it. I would sometimes imagine that the car had developed its own soul, forged from the experiences it had lived through with us; it had witnessed all our children growing up, it had seen my anger and pain. I was in it during some of my worst moments, when I was surely a hair's breadth away from going crazy. I had pounded on that car's steering wheel a thousand times, with the children screaming at me from the back to stop. I am sure it had secret autopilot powers and had helped me get from A to B when I was at my worst. The endless hours and miles that our car drove without a complaint, ferrying all the children to and from school, and between their activities, getting me to all my appointments safely, being a sanctuary for me sometimes, when I needed to cry for an hour alone, made it a real super car. That car was like another member of our family. (And in case you are wondering, at the time of writing my beloved car is still going strong, almost 25 years old!)

The only way I could cope, the only way I could get through the day and hit each intricately scheduled appointment, was to have my regime set in stone. By this time, I had reached to a point where, if I hadn't found an outlet for my sadness and frustration, I would have lost my mind, which is why I started meditating and walking every morning.

I started setting my alarm for 2:30 a.m. every day, when I would I get up and do a daily meditation, literally just praying for strength and sanity, help to get me through the day. Then I would spend some time in the bathroom getting ready. The bathroom, at this time of day, before anyone else got up, was my true sanctuary. I would light candles, a few tea lights, so it wasn't too bright, and then I would gently massage my body with warm massage oil, just to keep my muscles firm, and to keep my skin from toughening up.

Then at 4:00 a.m., I set out for a long walk. I liked walking in the dark at this time of the day. I felt connected to the universe, and the darkness seemed to give me some sort of protection and comfort. It was during these walks that I was able to do my own grieving and fully feel my pain, something I couldn't do in front of the children, or as I went about my busy daily schedule. I felt that this was the most appropriate time to release my grief; it was so early in the morning. I assumed that people would still be asleep and no one would hear me. I would walk and cry, letting everything out, voicing my fear and anguish, trying to let out all the anger and sadness.

I usually returned back to the house at around 5:00 a.m., then I would start preparing breakfast and whatever I was going to cook for lunch. The children got up by 5:30 a.m. to get on with their jobs; sweeping of the floors, both indoors and outdoors, hanging out laundry and laying the table for breakfast, feed the animals, cut fresh fruits from the garden. We ate breakfast together every morning at 6:30 a.m. during weekdays. After breakfast, the three older children would leave to catch their bus to school, while the younger two would get in the car, so I could drive them to school in Limassol. It was on the way back from this drop off that I stopped along the coastal road, near the Rock of Aphrodite, to go for my morning swim. I would be in and out of the water within 10 to 15 minutes, just enough time to really re-energise my body, before driving on, back to Paphos and opening the shop at 9:00 a.m. sharp!

Every day at 1:30 p.m., I would close the shop and start the school pick-up round. We ate lunch together around 3:00 p.m. and shared our news, before the afternoon schedule of classes started.

Dinner time was around 7:00 p.m., after the children had finished with their homework. They usually went to their rooms at around 9:00 p.m. after which I would do the last few chores around the house. I would fall into bed like a zombie at around 10:30 p.m. maximum.

I was surviving on four to five hours of sleep a night during those days!

Sometimes, when the schedule got really tight, Clara would lend a hand and drive the children to lessons, especially on a Saturday morning when I had to be in the shop. But otherwise, we managed alone. I say "managed," but I was honestly in that autopilot mode half the time.

On my morning walks, I felt so alone, so helpless. I was an orphan, a widow, my beloved brother had passed away two months after my husband. I felt more alone than I believed it was possible to be. I would repeat the words; "Help me, help me, help me," over and over. "Why?" I kept asking. "Why?" Why were all these terrible things happening to me? I imagined myself knocking on doors, pleading for help, begging anyone to help me, asking; "Who will help me? Please, someone help me!" I was sinking, deeper and deeper, into a black hole, and I didn't know how to get out of it. My heart was breaking apart. Every morning, I felt like another little piece of my heart had broken away.

One morning, while walking in the dark, I suddenly felt as if someone was following me. First, I was too scared to look back, but then I gathered all my courage and as I turned back, I saw our dog "Lassy" walking behind me. She must have sensed that something wasn't right with me. From that morning on, she was my steady companion on every single walk I did.

Clara was also very worried about me; she thought I was seriously risking my health by getting so little sleep. She couldn't understand why I was making myself get up at 2:30 a.m., why I didn't sleep more. I didn't really understand either; it just felt as I couldn't stop doing it. I was addicted to my routine. I needed to expel my grief every morning and clear my mind; it was the only way I could be ready to take on the day, otherwise I was convinced I wouldn't have made it through. Every morning I did my routine, over and over again. In some ways I guess it was like a kind of madness, but I couldn't see any way out. Every morning, before dawn, I set out on my walk, crying, shouting, pleading; "Please, help me, please, please…" I pleaded in vain, to the silent night air, until that particular morning when someone answered me.

I knew, it wasn't someone physically present, but it was more like a voice I heard inside my head. The voice said; "Everything is going to be okay. You are protected. You and your children are protected."

I remember exactly where I was when I heard this. I was at a T-junction in the road, at the highest point along my walk. I stopped dead in my tracks and looked ahead towards the ocean. The sun hadn't yet risen in the east and I was facing west; however, I remember seeing a beautiful light ahead of me.

Suddenly, everything felt different. I felt as if I was being bathed in warmth; I felt safe and calm. I heard the voice again; it was a soft voice, and I felt immediately comforted by a presence I felt nearby.

"You and your children are protected; everything will be alright." I couldn't distinguish whether the voice was old, young, male or female, it was as if it was a completely neutral sound, a voice like no other I had ever heard before. I felt as if an enormous strength had entered my body. I suddenly knew I would never be alone again. Filled with a new sense of peace, I started my journey home.

That was the turning point; that was the moment after which I became a strong force to be reckoned with. No one ever threatened us again after that morning. I never again felt consumed with fear or despair. Many things fell into place following that experience. I had read many spiritual books during my darkest days—I had literally been consuming them, and finally, I felt connected to something. From that moment on, whenever I needed an answer, I asked my inner voice. I calmly reached inside and waited for an answer.

I felt as though I had entered a different dimension, a higher state of consciousness; it was a dramatic shift. I suddenly had unshakeable faith that everything was going to be okay. My deep inner fear left me. I trusted my own intuition again, and I believed that someone, or something, somewhere, was supporting me. I am sure that, in only a few years, I must have grown spiritually, as much as others perhaps grow in an entire lifetime. I also finally understood that there is so much more to life waiting for us as soon as we are ready to embrace it.

Ironically, while giving me incredible strength, this experience also humbled me. I realised how ashamed I had been to feel so weak and helpless, that I had been too embarrassed to say— even to myself—that I couldn't cope, that I needed help. From that point on, I never felt too proud to ask for help, especially on a spiritual level. I would simply say out loud; "I don't know what to do here, please help me find the answer." Indeed, only the day after I had that life-changing experience during my morning walk, Clara said to me; "Regina, I think you should go and to see a healer. I feel that you need one; it's time to move on. You need to 'cut the cords' with your brother-in-law."

I wasn't too sure what she meant by "cutting cords," but still I went to the woman she suggested. This healer looked at me and she could tell I had been through some terrible stress. She started working on my body during our sessions, but for a few weeks, I felt nothing. Then one day, during a session, I felt something shift. By the next session, I was beginning to feel as though a huge weight was lifting off me. However, I still wasn't prepared for what the healer had in store for me. That day she said; "Today, we will 'cut the cords' with your brother-in-law, who is tightly connected to you." She told me that I had to imagine his presence and then say to him; "I love you, I am sorry, please forgive me, I let you go. Please go. I leave you." I had to keep saying these words whilst imagining his presence around me. At first, I thought; "What rubbish!" However, I did as she told me and at some point, I started to feel a little better.

Did I actually feel any forgiveness? No! I was only repeating what the healer had instructed me to say, but she told me I had to keep saying these words, every day, no matter what I felt. I was reluctant, but I told her that I would try.

The very next day, as I set off on my morning walk, I felt particularly angry. I walked quicker than usual and started crying—more with anger than sadness.

Suddenly I heard the voice again; "You must learn to forgive," it said.

"Why? Why should I?" I shouted back. I was furious, I didn't understand, why was I supposed to forgive the man who had caused my family and me so much pain, who had possibly caused the heart attack that had weakened my husband's heart. Why?

"You must forgive or you will be forever stuck," said the voice.

"Never!" I said out loud; "I will never forgive that horrible creature of a man, forget it! Never! I will never forgive that crazy man for what he put my children and me through! Never!"

"No, not him. Forgive Regina." Forgive "Yourself" said the voice inside me, and I stopped dead in my tracks.

Forgive. Lesson of new perspective. With tears rolling down my cheeks, I finally realised that it wasn't my brother-in-law I had to forgive for being so jealous of his younger brother Adonis, he just didn't know any better. But also, it wasn't my husband I had to forgive for dying and leaving me as a widow and the children as orphans. It was not even God, the Creator. All I had been asked for was to forgive myself. That moment, I remembered that I had made some stupid mistakes. I hadn't had the foresight to arrange for wills to be drawn up for my husband and myself earlier on. I had signed forms I didn't read nor understood. I had allowed myself to be afraid of everyone and everything. I lost faith in myself; I hadn't believed that I could stand up for myself and win.

In some way, looking at my role in the whole terrible mess helped me to forgive everyone else. Okay, my husband was also partly to blame for not thinking of making a will, but why didn't I ask him to? For fear that he would think it's unromantic, mercenary, or greedy even. In this, I had let my fear control me. And what could I really blame the in-laws for? I didn't know what their line of thinking had been. Perhaps, they felt that Adonis had mistreated them, had kept money from them. Both brothers worked for my husband, after all, and while I knew Adonis had been generous in giving his family pieces of land, perhaps they felt he had held the purse strings too tightly. Once they had access to the money, they did what they thought was right with it, even if I and everyone else thought it was wrong. And this "Power of Attorney" form that Nikos told me that Draco had in his possession. If he really had it, he obviously knew that he had obtained it through devious means, and to my knowledge, he had never actually used it.

I knew it was time to forgive everyone and move on. I still took some time and energy to work through and dispel that negative energy that surrounded my brother-in-law. In fact, it took few years before I felt completely free of the emotional connection to him. As I began to free myself from the emotions, my perspective changed, and I was able to see things from his point of view, and the first thing I thought about was how he must have felt when he had been judged by his own family.

I remember many years back, whenever I saw my "then" future mother-in-law she would ask me; "Haven't you got a nice girlfriend for my oldest boy, Draco?" She always asked, even in his presence. No wonder this man felt angry and resentful, with his mother repeatedly asking me, the girlfriend of his little brother, to find him a girl. She almost sounded desperate sometimes. How humiliating! In their family, tradition dictated that the men should find husbands for the girls. Draco was the oldest boy, and yet, here was his mother asking his little brother's girlfriend—a foreign girl, no less—to find him a girl.

Traditional Cypriot families often feel ashamed to have an unmarried child. My brother-in-law must have felt this deeply, and I imagine that this only fueled his resentment towards me. I remember asking him once; "Can't you smile, and say hello, just a few times?" He told me; "No." He then said; "This is who I am." And that was the end of it. I found that so hard to accept. I feel it's essential for everyone to experience and show some happiness in their lives.

I imagine most people, at some point in their lives, question themselves why they came into this world, asking; "What's my purpose? Why was I born into this family, to these parents? Why did I end up with these siblings, friends, relatives, etc.? Why was I born in this particular country and at this particular time?" Is it all just a random chance or is there some kind of purpose behind everything that happens? There is a saying that goes; "Life will never give you a burden you cannot carry." We all have lessons to learn and life will always throw us challenges, obstacles that stand in the way of our peace and happiness. Surely, it's our life's mission to learn how to navigate around or go through these challenges and grow. My brother-in-law was simply an obstacle in my life, a challenge that I had to go through and to overcome, in order to learn the lessons I was destined to learn.

Finally, the day came when I knew that whatever had kept me bound to my brother-in-law, to the man who had contributed to making my life an inferno, had gone. I literally felt free again. I began to live my life and enjoy myself again, free of resentment and anger, and free of fear.

I've often heard that "as soon as you are ready, doors open for you." That is exactly what I experienced. When I think back to those morning walks, when I cried and cried for days on end, I intuitively felt that before I can move on with my spiritual journey, I had to finish my grieving first. The day that I was ready for that turning point, a peaceful feeling descended upon me, and I knew that I am on the right path.

As my dear grandmother told me many times; "There is always a solution to any problem in life." We already know how to get the answers, but sometimes we aren't ready to hear or accept them. In our imagination, we construct scenarios that we think will solve our problems, but these aren't necessarily the way things will work out to be. Only when we are calm, at peace, and ready to accept, will we see the light.

I have experienced this so many times, thinking I have the answer and then finding out that I've gotten everything wrong. It wasn't until I experienced that turning point on my walk that I found the real way forward. After that point, I stopped looking for answers, I just quietly asked for help and the answers came to me. That was the point at which I knew the drama was over. Slowly, I moved on.

Over the next few years, I steadily healed myself. I also began to notice that people treated me differently. I felt respected instead of looked down upon. Perhaps, people only reflected back to me what I was starting to feel inside. The minute I lost all my fear and grounded myself in a strong belief that everything was going to be okay, that the children and I were protected, I also felt that people started to treat me differently. I could see it in their eyes; they respected me. Suddenly, rather than acting as if I didn't exist, people started enquiring as to how I was. People in our village, particularly the women, approached me to ask how things were going and how the children were doing, after all our struggles. People started respecting me as a woman, furthermore, as a foreign woman.

I felt as though I had been through a grueling military boot camp and now I had emerged, a survivor, wearing my badge of honor that said; "Here stands a woman who went to war unarmed, and never gave up."

PART THREE

Tradition. When I look back on all the problems I had with my in-laws in the years after my husband died, I find myself wondering if they all stemmed from the fact that I simply didn't behave in the way they felt a widow should behave. They had certain expectations based on their traditional views, and I wasn't playing ball.

Tradition plays an important role in our lives. Our traditional customs serve to bond people together; they help bridge the generational gap in families and enable people to feel connected to a particular culture. There is a comfort in familiarity and the repetition of long-standing rituals, like traditional festivals and celebrations. These have a valuable place in society. However, when traditions fly in the face of progress, when they are upheld dogmatically, even if they are outdated, they serve no one.

We live in an ever-evolving world; we cannot expect the same customs to serve us without any adjustments and updating as time goes on. We cannot expect to be observing the same traditions that were observed hundreds of years ago, if they obviously have no relevance in today's world. If we do, we will quickly stagnate. When young people feel limited and frustrated by the traditional expectations put upon them, they rebel, and this can cause friction in families and societies. Alternatively, they might conform, but then resent their elders for constraining them. Neither is productive, nor healthy. Our planet grows and evolves constantly, and so must we; it's the natural order of things.

Seeing the way in which my in-laws and other traditional Cypriot families uphold certain traditions, and the way these dogmatic views controlled the actions of young people, I couldn't help feeling that these customs potentially did more damage than good. I felt particularly strongly opposed to the tradition that women should be completely dominated by male family members, and subsequently their own husbands.

As I have built my life in Cyprus over time, I kept having the same conversation with local women. They constantly complained about the patriarchal society present on the island, but when I asked them why they didn't instigate for a change, they would throw up their hands and ask; "But what can we do? This is the way things are." In the early days, I would argue with them, urging them to be more proactive about bringing about change, but I soon realised that they had no intention of taking any action, that they were either too afraid or too weak. Or perhaps, secretly they didn't actually want a change anyway. So, I too joined their chorus of: "What can we do? This is the way things are!"

However, I never stopped feeling frustrated when I saw young people being trapped by their own old stubborn family members, into conforming to antiquated traditions and customs. I secretly prayed they would find the courage to break away and do things differently, at least make their own choices, even if they did decide that what they wanted was in line with those traditions. I saw some local children leave to go and study abroad as soon as they graduated from high school. I felt hopeful for them, that they would experience a different way of life. Indeed, they often returned with new, more progressive attitudes, but it didn't take long before they gave up their innovative and so-called radical ideas, and fell back into the old traditional ways of thinking.

I was determined that my children wouldn't be bound by outdated traditions; I was dedicated to raising open-minded children who were evolved and worldly. I wanted my children to be independent in thought and in spirit. The legacy I wanted to offer them was one that wasn't purely made up of money or real estate. I wanted to pass on to them as much knowledge as I could, to give them a wealth of experiences and to ensure they felt secure in the knowledge that they were loved, no matter what they chose to do.

Every country with its culture has different customs when it comes to heritage and wealth. In Austria, the tradition is that the man brings the house into the marriage, while the woman is responsible for equipping the house with all that is needed to run a household. Another Austrian tradition is that the eldest son is often expected to take over the family's house and business. In this way, the family name survives. If there are other siblings within the family, it's the eldest son's responsibility to pay his younger siblings their share of the inheritance, in money, land or whatever is available. In traditional families, the eldest boy often has no choice but to take over the family businesses, regardless of his own skills. If he cannot acquire the necessary skills quickly, the business may well go bankrupt. Those who inherit such burdens often feel unhappy about the situation, and this can obviously lead to problems down the line, primarily within the immediate family members.

In Cyprus, traditions differed from the ones I had known while I was growing up. For example, I discovered that in strict traditional Cypriot families, the woman's family is responsible for bringing the house into the marriage. The house would often be fully furnished and equipped, sometimes even down to a fully stocked refrigerator. Adonis with the support of his parents has built a house for most of his sisters before they got married. Perhaps, his family was disappointed that all he got was an Austrian girl with a couple of suitcases and a rented beach apartment! Most of Adonis' sisters had only been to elementary school; they were sent from young age to work in the fields to cultivate the family's land. The girls were very much kept in the background, behind their brothers.

When I first arrived in Cyprus, I was shocked to discover that some women from strict traditional families weren't allowed to go out alone without an escort. This would be their husband if they were married, or their brother or father if they weren't married. This was 1983! It was also the task of the parents or the boys in the family to find suitable men for the girls to marry.

In certain families, marriage is really like a business deal between the women's family and her future husband (and his family);

in many cases, women have no choice in the matter whatsoever. Her parents make all the arrangements, without consulting her, and as soon as the deal has been agreed (usually a mix of land, property and money), the woman is obliged to marry the man she has effectively been "sold" to. She might be allowed a brief discussion with her future fiancé, but this is a perfunctory exchange; in most cases, she doesn't have the right of refusal, she has to accept the terms her family has made. In some cases, the girl doesn't even set eyes on her husband until the day the deal is agreed upon. There is no mention of "love." It's primarily a business deal. Once the deal has been settled and all the marital arrangements have been made, the girl's family hosts a dinner only for close family members and the village priest, to celebrate and bless the engagement. The girl may then see her future husband, but no physical contact is allowed.

Traditions such as these suggest women are little more than the possessions of their fathers, a commodity to be bartered with. They then simply pass into the possession of their husbands. On the off chance a woman has the guts to refuse the man, she rarely gets another chance of an arranged marriage, and she brings shame on her family. Obviously, these marriage traditions date back to only the recent past of many countries in the world. In many developing and less progressive countries around the world, and in certain cultures, they are still very much in practice. But I was shocked to find evidence of such antiquated attitudes in the late twentieth century in Cyprus. I hadn't been in direct contact with people who upheld such outdated traditions before in my life.

So, no wonder Adonis' family was disappointed in his choice of me. I am sure they were hoping he would be approached by the father or brother of a well-respected local family, a family who had built their daughter a big house where the couple would live after holding a huge, traditional Cypriot wedding. They never openly voiced their dissatisfaction, but it was obvious from the way they looked and treated me that they were disappointed, mostly because of the fact that I didn't appear to add any material wealth to the family coffers. Indeed, I threatened it!

I felt their resentment and jealousy over the fact that I had taken away the most prolific provider in the family, the most successful and powerful family member, and certainly the most handsome male. He was a real asset to them, a prize, and he had gone to an orphaned foreigner. They must have resented the fact that I appeared to have come into the marriage empty-handed and yet could, one day, walk away with so much for myself and my children. Their nightmare began to come true when Adonis died; it often felt that the idea of me getting my hands on what they saw as their family heritage tortured them, sometimes even more than the loss of Adonis, an attitude I couldn't comprehend.

When I became a widow, it was expected that I would either marry again, to get a new protector (supporting me economically, so that Adonis' wealth could return to his family), or keep my status as a widow, but live under the "protection" of my late husband's family, with them controlling all the wealth. In this latter scenario, I would be expected to integrate into their family, obey their rules and wishes, and allow my children to be raised by them. Once it became obvious that I had no intention of either marrying again or handing over the raising of my children to anyone else, once they saw that I was serious in my intention to run my house and family by myself, it clearly angered them even further. They were never outspoken about how they felt, but they let me know in other ways, by trying to gain control of my children and heritage, mostly through illegal and immoral methods.

People sometimes ask me why I didn't just take the children and flee to Austria when things got so bad. I didn't do this simply because Cyprus was our home. I had fallen in love with Cyprus as I had fallen in love with my husband and kept falling in love with the place over and over again. There was never a question in my mind about leaving; it was my home and my children's home. Plus, technically, even though I didn't have access to it for some years, our inheritance was in Cyprus, and I needed it to raise my family and pay for their education. I wasn't going to turn my back on everything my husband had worked so hard for. He had always wanted to provide his family with a good and comfortable life, and it was now my responsibility to see that the children and I got that.

While I was growing up, I remember that my parents encouraged my brother to study architecture. They wanted him to go and work for our uncle who had a construction business. Everyone's hope was that my brother would one day go and open his own business. However, my brother's greatest ambition was to be a pilot. This was a fairly unattainable dream because in those days, where we lived, people needed to do practical work to earn a living. There was no money to train as a pilot. However, he was never happy with the profession my parents had steered him towards.

I had carved out a very different path. By saving money, I had the ability to choose exactly what I wanted to study and where I wanted to go; Paris! I broke free of my parent's control. My father couldn't stop me from pursuing my dream. Conversely, my brother battled against my parents and lost years of his life doing things he didn't have the desire or real ability to do. In the end, he rebelled and dropped out of the architecture course he had been enrolled in. That's when he moved to Germany and studied to become a sports car designer.

I never told my parents, but I felt they were wrong to control him so much when he was young; I felt that they had caused my brother great unhappiness. He was never truly happy with his life; it was as if he always felt he was living in someone else's shoes, that he wasn't living the life he had always dreamed of. He was wise and deeply spiritual, and I feel he never reached his full potential.

When my brother called me a few months before he died, he was already in the hospital. We spoke on the phone for hours that day, and although I didn't know at the time that it would be our very last conversation, I could feel it was an exceptionally meaningful one. At the start of our conversation, he wished me a happy 50th birthday, which was a week or so away, and then he said that he had something important to tell me.

Firstly, he really opened up about how he had felt when we were young, how he really felt when he was forced into doing something he didn't want to do. In hindsight, I realise that he probably knew he was dying, that was why he was really opening up to me. Then he explained that he wanted to encourage me not to make those mistakes with my children. He was just offering a few words of advice, a little bit of wisdom for me to think about, as I guided my then young children through their lives.

"My dear sister," he said. "Your children are so young still. When the time comes for them to go out into the real world, allow them to do whatever they want to do with their lives. The universe will guide them. Don't worry. You will have done your job as a mother; you can set them free. They all have strong instincts and those instincts will guide them." I never forgot my brother's words. While I tried to teach my children everything they would need to know on a practical level, I encouraged them to make their own decisions about what paths they wanted to follow.

I ensured that my children spoke four languages pretty much fluently. I taught them to be responsible for their own spaces, their own rooms, and all their possessions. I taught them all how to cook, so that they would grow up to be independent. They were all responsible for their own money, their pocket money; they learnt how to save it and make good choices regarding how to spend it. During the school holidays, they all worked to make some extra money, either doing carpentry, or at a car-wash station, or any odd job that was available to them. I always encouraged them to earn their own money. However, I never tried to steer them towards one profession or another, influence their choices of what to study, of what career paths to follow, these were purely their own. I only helped to guide them towards what they wanted; I didn't impose my will on them in that respect.

The children understood and saw the sacrifices I made in order to run the household and ensure our lives were clean and healthy, and they learnt that they had to make sacrifices too.

What I taught them actually gave them far more liberation in the future than many of their friends had. During the summer holidays when they were old enough, I sent them to foreign countries to mix with other cultures and learn about other nationalities and traditions, to further broaden their minds. And as each of them finished with their high school education, I took them traveling, to help them decide where to go to for University, and to give them some unique experiences. My children have traveled through Europe, India, Australia, New Zealand, South America and South Africa. I gave them freedom to explore the world, and I taught them that it was essential to take responsibility for their own lives. They have all gone off in different directions, and I am immensely proud of all their achievements. Today, they all seem so happy with their academic studies and careers they have chosen to pursue, and I am eternally grateful to my brother for his last, departing wise words to me. I know these words helped me make the right decisions in life.

Most importantly, I believe I taught my children about the importance of love and respect, and about the discipline required to live a healthy life.

Why? Why did I write this book? I feel that it's the right time to share my life's experiences with you, so that, hopefully, you might be spared from going through such struggles as I went through. Now, looking back, I can say that there was nothing normal throughout my entire life, everything that happened to me was so unexpected and unusual. Whenever I kept asking myself; "Why, why all this happens to me?" I just couldn't find the right answer for it! Even me, considering myself as a rock-solid, grounded person, being gifted with a strong will and a sharp perception, but still, there were times that I literally had lost the ground below my feet.

Surely, we all make mistakes throughout our lives, but the mistakes that I made, especially after my husband's passing, weren't only a huge cost to me, in terms of health and wealth, but also to my children. Some of the decisions I made, were no one's fault but solely my own "*mea culpa*." I was innocent and naive, and so, I paid the price. I dearly hope that this book will save you from unnecessary pain by learning from my mistakes.

Firstly, here is my most important piece of advice. If you are a husband, or a wife, or a parent, it's absolutely a must to make a will. First of all, be aware that "innocence and naivety" are, in no country, protected against laws and regulations. Even if you live in a fair, democratic country and have the most wonderful in-laws, I encourage you to always make a will! If you share something with someone—could be a property or even a child, you must make sure that you have stated what you want to happen to your share in the event of your passing away. To do otherwise, to sit around and pretend you are never going to die is delusional and selfish. Of course, no one wants to believe that they will die tomorrow, but the point is that death is a certainty. At the end of the day, it's part of our life cycle. We will all die, and it could happen at any time. If you have no will, even if there are no meddling in-laws or corrupt officials in your life, then your loved ones will experience more trauma and upheaval than it's necessary after you have gone.

Secondly, if you are a husband, make sure your wife understands the fundamental responsibilities and duties you take care of. If you are a wife, make sure your husband understands the fundamental responsibilities you take care of, and at least to run the household. No one should be doing tasks that nobody else knows about. Imagine what would happen if one day you didn't come home to do that essential task, and no one else knew it needed to be done. Everything would fall apart. Imagine how traumatizing that would be to a child, on top of the fact that they had just lost a parent. Ensure that both of you know how everything operates. When I hear a husband or wife say; "Oh, I know nothing about that, my husband/wife takes care of all of that," I cannot help thinking; "No! Don't live like that, because if that partner passes away suddenly, on top of the terrible, debilitating grief you would suffer, you wouldn't know how to keep your life and even less your family going." Be responsible; be loving. Think about what your partner or your children would go through if you were to die tomorrow.

My next piece of essential advice is to never sign anything you haven't read and understood. You might assume you would never do this. Well, so did I! I was no fool; I was an intelligent, educated woman, and yet I went ahead and signed forms that I hadn't fully understood. When your world is shattered and your emotions are running high, it's amazing what decisions you make when you aren't in your right mind. Be honest, have integrity, but never assume that others will have the same high principles as you do. Today, all my affairs are in order. I have a watertight will and my children are all aware of its exact context. They all have separate financial accounts, and I have an individual file for each of them. They have everything that is supposed to be rightfully theirs, in their names. When I depart from this life, there will be no need for expensive lawyers and courtroom dramas; there will be no need for any difficult discussions; everything is stated in black and white. At least, this is what I am hoping for as corruption still exists.

Finally, love your enemy. He or she is your greatest teacher in life. One of the most important lessons I learnt, through the years of all these struggles, is that anger, bitterness and fear aren't your best weapons when you have a fight on your hands. This may sound strange, but if you try to love and understand your enemy, you may see solutions that are hidden behind that big wall of rage. In the end, your best weapon is love, not aggression towards these individuals.

Another thing I would like to encourage you to do is to be there for people during their grieving. Bereavement is an incredibly lonely place. I felt so isolated after the death of my husband, but when I found myself wondering why people didn't call round or inquire how I was doing, I remembered how I had once failed myself in this respect.

Some neighbours of ours had four children, the wife was pregnant with the last one, also being a boy. They had four boys and were trying one last time for a girl. Tragically, the wife passed away during the childbirth and her husband was left with five children to look after on his own; the exact situation I found myself two years later. Did I go and visit him, or ask him if there was anything I could do for him? No, I didn't. I couldn't find the right words to say. That's the problem; people don't know what to say when something so tragic happens, so they avoid making contact. Death is something so frightening to most people that they want to avoid any conversation about it. I never found the courage to approach my neighbour because I couldn't think of what to say. I felt terrible about it when I found myself in the same situation, but I still didn't approach him! Indeed, by then I had my own traumatic events to deal with, I certainly had no time for anyone else. Several years later, I finally apologised to him for not visiting or offering any help. He told me not to worry, that he completely understood and was sorry he hadn't come to offer me any support either.

Hopefully, from simply reading this book, it has taught you something about bereavement. Of course, it's difficult to know what to say, especially when you haven't experienced bereavement yourself, people are so sensitive when they are going through grief; it's a very delicate situation, but they almost always do need support.

I count my blessings for Clara, who always instinctively knew what I needed. She wouldn't make it a big deal out of anything. She would leave some flowers or a cake, or some small gifts by the door and then leave. She would come in, help the children with their homework and then leave. She helped teach the children small things, like writing 'thank you!' cards for gifts they received from friends and family. She took care of so many of the small details that I didn't have time for. I was worrying about the big issues, like getting by, financially, like soothing the children through their grief, and fighting for what was rightfully ours/theirs.

The children also became my best friends through our years of struggle, and I feel they became very mature from the experience.

Ultimately, though, I feel that it wasn't Adonis' death that caused us so much pain, but what happened following this, with all the actions of my in-laws that made life so intolerable at times. Death isn't dark; it's sad, but it's not dark. What was dark was the fear of being pushed into a corner with no options, by the actions of people I couldn't control; what was dark was being afraid that I would never get justice. What was dark was the constant interference in our lives, the manipulation and threat of our basic rights. A family member had changed the birth certificates of the children and had got away with it. If the authorities could let something like this happen, I can't imagine what else was possible. We felt threatened by corruption. We felt our safety and unity was threatened at its very core.

It would have been so easy to let things go, to start drinking perhaps, or give up; it would have been easy to lie down in defeat, to let the house go, to let everything slip. But this never entered my mind. I had to keep going; I was driven by the mere instinct of survival. Also, I believed that if I slipped up for one second, then the in-laws would have pounced on me and got me declared as an unfit mother. I feared of losing my children more than anything.

I think of my children as five precious diamonds; each of them has played their own essential role in my life, especially during my years of pain and struggle. I think of them as diamonds because their experiences have shaped them, in the way a diamond gets shaped by all the pressures around it, over time. They had so much put upon them, and yet they all ended up so uniquely beautiful. Thankfully, they are all doing so well; it's a miracle that they are all following their path so well, considering what they went through their teenage years.

Having five children was always going to be interesting. I knew that each child would be unique. They were all wanted and loved so deeply by their father and myself, and I have always been immensely proud of having such a large family. From a very early age, each one of them showed their individuality and strength of character. I brought them to this world, and I helped to feed and shelter them, but they created their own visions and desires. They were incredibly mature and responsible, even as young children; there were no major "teenage issues" to sort out. Really! Sometimes, I felt as if they were born adults, as if they already had huge wisdom and maturity; it was an honor to raise such wonderful people. I am proud of all of them, to this day, and I know they will continue to make me proud, throughout their lifetimes. They have all grown into such interesting souls, each of them forging their own path in life.

They have always been, and always will be, my best blessing in life.

At the time of writing this book; after graduating with a degree in Computer Science and Technology from a University in the U.K., Markos has also achieved his ambition and has qualified as a professional airline pilot. He is so focused and well organised, I feel he is particularly well suited to this profession; he has a calm and practical mind. Eva, as the oldest girl, continues to be the 'heart of the family' and everyone still goes to her with their troubles and personal secrets. She is studying criminal law at a University in the U.K., a profession perfectly suited to her passionate nature and sense of justice, and also maintains her keen interest in politics and international relations. Diogenis becomes more and more like his father. He has a huge personality. He is full of ideas and is infinitely ambitious. He just graduated from a University in the U.K. and is working towards having an international business career. Adonis Jr. is still the most sensitive and gentle soul of the five of them, the introspective one. He is really enjoying University life in Australia, studying for a degree in Wildlife Science. Cleopatra, the baby girl, is strong-willed and independent; sometimes I think she is a carbon copy of me. She is always cheerful, but there is a deep purpose in everything she does. Of all the children, she excels best in languages, and I have no doubt she will become a successful international journalist, as she hopes to become when she graduates from her University in France.

These days, with all my children spread far and wide across the world, I relish the times we are all together, which happens mostly during the Christmas or Easter holidays, and sometimes during the summer months.

My children have never been afraid to speak up to me or to challenge me, but they do so with respect. I have always spoken to them with respect, so they respect me back. They know I make up the house rules, and they abide by them, but I don't make the rules of their hearts. Their opinions and feelings are their own. Of course, as their mother, I think I know them; I believe I know what to expect from them, but in fact, the more certain I am that they will make this choice, or that choice, the more likely it's that they surprise me. They are a constant source of information and fascination for me.

As parents, I don't believe we have the right to expect something back from our children. We can guide them, but we must let them go at some point. I learnt this once, by watching our chickens roam free in our house garden. Interestingly, the mother hen was looking after her chicks when they were still young; they followed her around and she found food for them. One day, they escaped, under the fencing. The mother hen couldn't follow them because she was too big, but she called them back and they came back to her. A few hours later, they escaped again. This time, they found their own food and began pecking it. When the mother hen saw this, she knew that they were independent. She realised that they could find food for themselves, that they could survive on their own, so she knew her job as a protective and caring mother was done. What she did next was extraordinary to witness. She completely changed her voice, and then, she even changed the color of her feathers, from dark brown to light brown, so that her chicks couldn't recognise her, and assumed they were alone. It sounds cruel, but that's just how nature works. The chicks came looking for her, but she did nothing to identify herself. It was her way of making them understand that they were now independent.

While I get such joy from watching my children grow and develop, I know my job as their mother changes as they become more and more independent, and I try not to put too much pressure on them. It feels as if in life, the role of parenthood is adopted while bringing up children, in order to guide them through life and help them establish a solid foundation before they take off.

I now come back to those questions I mentioned earlier; the questions that most of us find ourselves asking at some point during our lives: Who am I and what is my purpose here? What is my legacy? What do I leave behind after this lifetime? I believe we all have two missions to fulfil; one is at a personal level, and the other is at a global level. We are ought to fulfil these missions if we want to move on with our lives. These questions are fundamental and existential. By looking deep inside ourselves and asking these questions, this will trigger us to start to develop as individuals, spiritually.

Now you may ask, what does it matter whether I develop spiritually or not? Or, what good does it do to move forward and grow spiritually? Well, if you decide to stay where you are at, if you decide not to improve yourself, if you are satisfied with your daily struggles, with the problems you encounter over and over again, then maybe you do not need to grow spiritually, but then what is the point of living? Isn't the point of living to grow? All living things are born, grow and then die, in a single natural life cycle. Thus, when we stop growing and learning, then we are at the final phase of this cycle, isn't it?

Many people don't like to take responsibility for their actions. They don't like challenges. They believe life owes them everything. This is clearly an "one-way" road. For those people, life will never change; it will be a constant struggle, unfortunately.

However, should you belong to the category of people who want to move on, and don't shy at hard work, as well as willing to take risks, then life will open new doors for you.

Whatever it is you may need, it's my pleasure to help you along on your life's journey, whether it's self-worth, confidence, self-love, inner strength or even some kind of motivation. All you need is to ask for help, and it will be given.

As the proverb says; "When the student is ready, then the teacher appears."

Year 2013. Revelation of new experiences and lessons. The irony of what happened to me in March is so ludicrous, you can only laugh. After you cry!

In November 2012, nine years after the start of the issue with the big multinational company, my Third Lawyer finally managed to secure a court date. We had set many meetings previously, to which no one had turned up, and she had exhausted all her efforts in trying to get them to settle out of court, so this was the last resort. In fact, it was a few years since she had first secured a court date for the hearing, but the company kept postponing it; they were so powerful, even the legal system bowed down to them. Finally, the court threatened them that if they didn't turn up; a ruling would be made. So, another new date was set and we turned up ready for a legal fight.

Before we entered the courtroom, however, a middle-aged man approached me and asked me my name. He introduced himself as the General Manager of the company. He shook my hand and told me I was a very tenacious woman, and that he admired my strength. Then, without hesitation, he took out his cheque book and asked me how much the company owed me. I was really astonished, as I didn't expect such action! Therefore, I passed on to him the paper that my accountant has given me, with the total outstanding amount.

He made a full and final cheque payment for all the back rent, as well as the legal expenses I had incurred over the past nine years. The court hearing had been resolved just outside the court room, and that was the end of this ongoing case. My lawyer explained that we could probably have got more if we had forced them into court, but I had seen enough courtrooms in my life, so I was content to take what we had agreed at first hand.

I had never seen such a large sum of money on a check. As the trustees of my husband's estate, the children and I were equal recipients of that money, and it was supposed to be split into six ways. By that time, the children all had their own accounts and once the check had been cleared in my account, I intended to distribute the funds into six equal shares. However, the bank manager explained that it would be simpler to leave the entire sum in my account, until the appropriate taxes had been cleared, which would take a few months to be processed.

If I would have split them into the different accounts from the beginning, we would still have the majority of it now. As it happened, thanks to the "Great Cyprus Bank Robbery" of March 2013, most of it was gone, and I was still locked into a legal battle with the government, along with many other unfortunate Cypriot residents, trying to recover their rightful capital.

I felt like a complete fool. How could this have happened again? What was it with me and money? Was I destined to let money slip through my fingers for the rest of my life? Did I have some "karmic debt" to pay that was related to money? I didn't know the answers to these questions, but I knew one thing had to change. This time I wasn't going to let the loss of money depress me. I refused to let this incident crush me like the previous times.

(Really, you have to wonder if there is a subversive legacy of taking things in Cyprus. The British took Cyprus, and then the Turks took a big part of it. No wonder our leaders thought they could simply take people's savings. No wonder my in-laws thought they could just take my husband's rightful and hard-earned heritage!)

The worst of it all was that Diogenis, who was studying at a University in the U.K. at the time, had been warning me that something like this was going to happen in the near future. Ever since the elections in Greece the previous summer, these had brought in more austerity measures and created problems between the Greeks and the EU. Diogenis had warned me that Cyprus was also in trouble. So, I hated having to tell him that we had lost the majority of the money. I felt physically sick as I explained that most of the money had gone, and I think he was struggling to hold back his tears as he listened to me. But in the end, I told him it's only money. All that really mattered to me was that my children were safe and well, and thriving in their personal pursuits in life, that they had all grown into interesting, intellectual, compassionate human beings who were going to do great things in this world. Of that, I was certain! "Not only that," I said; "Just take a look at my life. I am living in a beautiful house, in a beautiful country that, despite all the troubles, I still love; a place I will always call home. I still consider myself an extremely fortunate person." I don't know if I was helping Diogenis, but I was certainly making myself feel better as I spoke. "Be happy for me," I told him. "We are all going to be just fine." And I believed this, and I still do.

When I got off the phone with Diogenis, I decided to go to my favourite spot for a swim. I got into the car and drove out to the Rock of Aphrodite, the place where I had fallen in love with my husband and had sealed my fate, setting the course for the rest of my life.

Look where I have come, I thought, as I drove. Here I am, a widow, a survivor, a mother. All my children are doing well, living independently away from home, working or studying at University. I have a good home and a decent income. Never mind the money I had lost, I thought, never mind the troubles I had faced, all that was over now. Suddenly, at the age of 61, I felt as if I had the whole of my life ahead of me.

I shivered with excitement.

Every time I stopped by the Rock of Aphrodite to go for a swim in the past, I always parked my car in a space by the side of the road. I crossed the road and climbed over the low barrier, between the side of the road and the rocks that led down to the beach. I must have followed this routine literally hundreds of times.

This time, however, when I got out of my car, I noticed, for the first time, that there was actually a set of steps leading down from the car park to a tunnel that ran under the road, so that people could access the beach safely (and not cross the old highway road). I had no idea if this had just been built, or if it had always been there, all along, but I was curious to investigate, and so I did.

At the bottom of the stairs, I peered down the tiny, narrow tunnel; it was just wide and tall enough for a single person to walk through, quite carefully. The tunnel's wall had been reinforced with the sand-colored stone, typical to Cyprus. Because it was so narrow, it was quite dark, so I started walking carefully through it, towards the little patch of light I could see at the end of it.

"There it is," said a voice in my head. "There's the light at the end of the tunnel." I started to weep. As I made my way towards the light, big tears of joy ran down my face. I held my hands together and pressed them against my heart.

"Thank you, my darling," I said to Adonis. "Thank you for bringing me here. I couldn't have done it without you." I walked on, almost blinded by tears. I could hear the soundtrack to our first night of love. Ahead of me was the sound of the waves, softly lapping against the pebbled beach. I knew when I emerged into that blessed white light, my old life would be left behind, and my new life would have begun. I felt the chains breaking, and the weight lifting off me; I knew the last of it was now gone for good. I closed my eyes, and took that last step, and I emerged into the white light, and never looked back ever again.

THE END

Afterword

My Learnings. I wanted to say a few words, outside of the main story of the book, more about what I have learnt from my experiences in life. I have come to believe that we are all here for a reason, and that is therefore a reason why everything that happens to us, actually happens. I believe that we all have a purpose to fulfil, but we have many lessons to learn before we can fill the roles destined for us. Unfortunately, these lessons are often painful and necessitate a great deal of suffering. Some people never get past the suffering stage; they get stuck in that place of pain. We often don't realise that we have been suffering in order to learn some vital lessons, until some time has passed, and we have perspective. It took me a few years to appreciate the lessons I was being taught through my life experiences, and to understand why I had to go through everything I went through, but I got there eventually. I finally came to understand the reasons why I had been through these experiences.

The knowledge I've gained through my experiences hasn't only transformed me as a person, but it has also transformed my life in so many ways. Even though I've had to learn the hard way, today, I can honestly say that I am grateful for everything that life has taught me. I am grateful for all the people who have come into my life, still living or now deceased; for those who caused me pain, as well as those who nurtured me, because they have all been my teachers. Each person has contributed, in one way or another, to the person I have become today. Of course, I am particularly grateful to the mentors and spiritual teachers who gently guided me and supported me when I was in the darkest hours of my suffering.

I believe I was destined to learn three key lessons in life. When I look at what all my painful experiences taught me, it's clear to me that the key lessons I was being taught were **forgiveness** (how to forgive myself as well as others), **trusting my intuition** (having the courage to make my own decisions rather than letting others control my life) and **asking for help** (from both the physical and spiritual worlds).

I can pinpoint three significant experiences from my life's journey that relate to each of these lessons.

When I think about my lesson in **forgiveness**, I believe it came in the form of my relationship with my brother-in-law. He was my tormentor for many years. Why? When I look back I can see that we were linked in a way I struggled to understand. It was as if I simply couldn't break free from him. It was only when I fully forgave him that my life began to improve. Through this, I also came to forgive myself and my husband for leaving us without having things put in order. There was something almost spiritual in the way I was shackled to my brother-in-law, and I think the first time I came to understand it was when I had a series of dreams that occurred in January 2010. It was long after I had broken free from him, but they seemed to explain much about my relationship with him that I hadn't fully appreciated before.

I am not a person who dreams much, or at least, I don't remember many of my dreams. In fact, before this series of dreams, the only dream I remember is the one I had about a year or so after my husband had passed away. In it, the children and I were sitting at dinner and my husband walked into the room. He hugged and kissed us all and told us he loved us. I could feel his lips on mine, and I clearly heard his voice; there was so much love and tenderness in it. This dream reassured me that love never ends, that wherever my husband's spirit is, he will always love us. It gave me so much strength and hope, and helped me cope with life at that stage.

The series of dreams I had in January 2010 were much darker; in fact, it would be more accurate to call them nightmares!

There were three dreams in total, and they took place over the course of about a week. In the first dream, I was a young, beautiful Arabic girl living in some Middle Eastern country, maybe 100-150 years ago. I was a slave being held by a wealthy family. One of the male members of the family was badly abusing me and eventually killed me. Just before I died, I vowed to come back and haunt him, saying I would get my revenge for what he had put me through. As I died in the dream, I woke up. I felt terrible. My stomach was in knots and all I wanted to do was vomit. I was also desperately saddened by the fact that there was no one there to hold my hand. The feeling of loneliness and isolation was the worst part; the sense of aloneness was almost unbearable. I was both terrified and devastated, and at the same time, filled with a feeling of hatred. It was one of the worst feelings I had ever had, waking up so abruptly.

In the second dream, I was sitting in the audience of a packed cinema watching a movie. Suddenly I saw myself on screen. I'm not sure what the details of the plot were, but I knew my on-screen character was the reincarnation of this Arabic girl, and that I had lived through many lifetimes. I was playing a role where I was searching for my enemy, who I knew was the abuser from my first dream. I was preparing myself to fight him, I was gathering my strength, but I was also running out of time. Before I could find him and get my revenge, I woke up. I felt so angry. Just when I thought I was going to be able to punish him, after searching for him through many lifetimes, the dream was abruptly interrupted. I woke with such a deep sense of sadness and emotional imbalance. I was so crushed by the feeling of disappointment that I hadn't found my abuser and punished him. I found it very difficult to go about my daily life for the next few days.

Finally, a few nights after that second dream, I dreamed the final installment in this dream series, and finally the relevance was revealed. In the dream, in which I was another character in another lifetime (but again, the details were unclear), I knew I was going to meet my abuser, but just before I did, I met another man. This man was very tall and handsome with piercing green eyes and dark blonde hair. I immediately fell in love with him, and then discovered that he was the brother of my abuser. Finally, this dark soul appeared and I knew this was the man I had been searching for. He looked like Dracula, with dark hair and sunken eyes. He was tall and thin, with some missing teeth and pale skin. His mouth was downturned at the corners, and he looked as though he had never smiled in his life. I was shocked to see what complete opposites these two brothers were.

Within my dream, I instinctively knew that this almost inhumane creature had suffered terribly all his life, that he had experienced nothing but misery. On the one hand, I felt victorious at having found my enemy after many lifetimes of searching, and I could feel all of my hatred rising up inside me, but I also felt such pity for him. Here I was preparing to get my revenge and make him suffer, but yet, I intuitively felt that he had experienced pain through every life he had lived. He was almost a shell of a man. I sensed that he had already been punished and it wasn't my place to punish him further, that I wasn't there to be the judge or executioner. I suddenly knew that my only task was to forgive him. At first, it was a strange feeling, to forgive this man who had hurt me so badly, but the more I accepted it, the better I felt. Even within my dream, I could literally feel the weight lifting off me and, as it did, I turned to look at the handsome brother, the man I loved, and felt completely content. With the relief I felt at having forgiven my tormentor, I realised that I should have forgiven him many years earlier. If I had, I wouldn't have needed to experience all the anguish I had felt through all my lifetimes; the hatred, and the need for revenge. I had been emotionally imbalanced for so long, but now I had forgiven this soul and taken the thorn out of my side; I knew I could heal and move on.

When I woke up from this dream, I felt an overwhelming sense of peace and understanding. Obviously, these men represented my husband and brother-in-law, but the dream gave me a new perspective. I understood that my brother-in-law had only acted the way he had because he was suffering. He was desperate, whereas I had this wonderful husband, the love of my life.

When I forgave that poor soul in my dream, I had felt such lightness and joy, as the weight of hatred, and the need for revenge was lifted from my shoulders. I thought of the saying; "Forgive and you will be forgiven." I experienced this directly. I was able to go much further into my self-forgiveness after this moment. It was fascinating that it had taken me several lifetimes to understand that had I forgiven my brother-in-law earlier, I could have moved on with my life rather than experience so much distress. To forgive him had always been within my power, but it had taken me years to realise this.

Since fully understanding this lesson, I have always practiced forgiveness, building it into my daily life and meditations, as well as keeping a sense of it about me at all times. I have found that, as a result, my life is filled with peace, joy and happiness.

Learning to **trust my intuition** rather than let others control my life was probably the hardest lesson I had to go through. A recent experience I had with one of my children really highlighted this lesson to me.

My son, Markos, was searching for a new apartment in Vienna, Austria. He had sent me some information on a few he was looking at and asked for my opinion. I told him which one he should choose and that he should take it immediately. He quickly sent me a message saying; "Thanks for your kind advice, Mum. I'll make my own decision when the time is right." I felt a mix of feelings when I read his message. On the one hand, I was impressed that my son trusted his own instincts and was prepared to set a boundary with me, saying that he wasn't automatically going to do what I told him, that he was going to digest my advice and act when he felt he knew what he wanted. On the other hand, I felt really sad to think of how many times I hadn't said something along these lines to someone when I should have done. In some areas of my life, like when I decided to move to Paris to study, or when I made decisions about how to raise my children, I had been very strong and listened to my intuition. But after my husband died, I lost my way. When someone told me what to do, I often didn't stand up for myself. Sometimes, I gave the impression that I was asserting myself, but in actual fact I had no true belief in what I was doing and saying at the time.

I was immensely proud of my son for standing up to me. I think parents often try to force their opinion and will onto their children. When we do that, we do them a disservice. We should be teaching them to trust themselves, to trust their own instincts, to believe that they will always know what is right, deep down, that they don't need someone else to tell them what is right.

I firmly believe that we are all born with strong intuition. We simply have to learn to listen to it. When I look back at all the times I hadn't listened to my own gut instincts but had done what others asked me to do, I realised that my actions came from fear, a fear of upsetting people or "getting it wrong." I was basically afraid that a) people would abandon me or punish me if I didn't do as they wished, and b) that I wouldn't be able to work out by myself on what was best for me. It all came down to a lack of self-trust. My son's actions highlighted to me that people aren't offended when you assert your own will (or at least if they are, it shouldn't be as important as doing what you feel is right). I wasn't in the least bit offended by my son's words. Quite the opposite, I was proud of him for being so forthright and strong, and a little ashamed of myself for thinking it was okay to be so forceful and opinionated with him. And I felt a certain wistful joy that he was teaching me this lesson. I do believe that we choose our parents before we are born, we choose them for the lessons we can learn from them and the lessons we can teach them. I even think we choose the environment we are born into because there are lessons within those specific boundaries that we need to acquire. My son certainly contributed into teaching me an important lesson I needed to learn.

Even though it was a very quick and simple message, reading what my son wrote really brought home to me how powerless I became after my husband died. I reflected on how, until his death, I had been a very strong woman. I was opinionated, determined to succeed and focused. I had made decisions with my husband about how to run our household and raise our children. I was rock solid. But losing him, and going through all the traumatic events that followed, had sapped all my power. I felt numb, as if I couldn't make any decision myself, let alone the right decision. If anyone pushed me, I would bend. It was like I lost touch with my intuition. How different would my life have been if I hadn't lost that power? Why had I become so weak?

When I thought deeply about it, I realised that even before all the drama of my husband's death there had been times in my life when I hadn't felt able to assert myself, for fear of offending someone. Why did I have to go through so much pain and hardship before learning to trust my intuition, before learning to say "no" to people? Was I really so afraid of offending them? I think it may have been partly because I had been raised to be polite. I grew up in a time when we were taught to respect the opinions and decisions of our elders, when it wasn't acceptable to challenge them. Maybe I had learnt to be submissive, regardless of what was right for me. I now see that this can be detrimental, and I want to pass this message on to others, including my own children (which, certainly in Markos' case, I seem to have done successfully!). I want to tell others that they must exercise the right to do what feels best for them. It took me years of turmoil and emotional instability to understand this, and I certainly don't want anyone else to go through what I went through.

This really was a huge lesson for me. I hadn't just started to distrust my intuition, but I had literally let go of my life. The worst part of my whole experience was seeing how rapidly things can spiral downwards once you relinquish control of your life. I felt like things started going from bad to worse, and the whole process accelerated until I was in the deepest and darkest hole you could imagine. I will never forget what that felt like.

The point I want to make is that we all have intuition. We all innately know what is right and what is wrong for us, but so many of us don't access it or pay attention to it. We listen to other voices, we drown out our own voice, or we have our own voice silenced by someone. If we want to live true to our purpose, true to what is right, true to our integrity, we must learn to tune in to that intuitive voice and let it guide us.

Sometimes, you can have strong intuition in one area of your life (perhaps in business dealings) and distrust your intuition in another area (say relationships), and we will all have different teachers for different areas of our lives. Personally, one aspect of my life that I feel I did get right, intuitively, was my role as a mother. I laid the foundation for each of my children to have a strong sense of self. I encouraged them to trust themselves and to make their own decisions so that later on in life they don't become dependent on others, or let others take control of their lives. I taught them to be independent and strong. I taught them to consider their options when any decision had to be made, and not to rush any big decisions. I told them they should always try to sleep over important decisions because they would usually have greater clarity in the morning. They have all followed my advices. I never needed to tell them what was right or wrong. I always asked them to think for themselves. When we, as parents, tell a child that something is "wrong," we are taking away their ability to attune to their intuition. Figuring out what is "wrong" by listening to their own intuition helps children to trust their instincts and helps them to mature and become independent. In other words, don't teach them what we think is wrong, teach them to think for themselves and decide for themselves what is wrong.

Learning to use your intuition is like learning to drive a car. It takes practice. Everything we learn in life takes time, so the sooner you start, the better.

The third big lesson I learnt through the course of all my struggles was how to **ask for help**. This is a lesson I believe most people really struggle to learn. Why does it feel so uncomfortable to ask for help? Perhaps because it makes us feel weak and powerless, as if we somehow belittle and diminish ourselves by asking. And I am not just talking about asking for help from our friends and family, I have also come to believe that, in times of trouble, we need to ask for spiritual help. No matter what you believe in, whether you are religious or not, praying for help and guidance from the spiritual world is especially essential when you find yourself lost and confused.

It often happens, and especially in the western world, that people are reluctant to ask for help because they are scared that the person they ask assistance from will one day expect something in return and they don't want to be in anyone's debt. I've never really subscribed to this concept, even though I am familiar with it. Although, I was raised in a time when children were expected to look after their parents in old age, I believe that parents shouldn't have such expectations of their children as this sense of expectation and entitlement doesn't contribute to an unconditional and healthy bond. I rather support the idea of being a parent is a privilege. Our children don't owe us; they aren't in our debt because we gave them life and raised them—we have done so freely. I love my five children and I wholeheartedly did so much for them, but they didn't ask this of me, I chose to have them and raise them. I don't ever want them to feel obliged to take care of me "in return." If they want to look after me in my old age, that would be wonderful, but I don't carry this as an expectation, or put pressure on them. I am sure many people—both parents and children—would be much happier if they embraced this idea.

In ancient times, the concept of love always had two meanings. "Eros" was the word given to physical love (and, of course, also the God of Love), and "agape" was the word that referred to the type of unconditional love a mother has for her child. For any relationship to work, in the long term, you need both. You start with the physical love (whether this is the attraction to a partner or the attraction to a baby because it's cute and adorable), but then you have to develop the "agape" love, the unconditional love, because this is what will sustain you and enable you to support and care for that special someone. When you love someone like this, you give freely; you don't expect anything in return.

There are stories about King Solomon (who lived around 900 BC) that quote him as saying the love a mother has for a child is the most powerful force in the universe, which is why he believed that women were ultimately more powerful than men.

I believe unconditional love is what our planet needs most.

When I question why I was always so reluctant to ask for help from anyone or anything, again I have to go back to my childhood and analyse how I was raised. Just as I was raised to be polite and not offend people, which I now feel compromised my ability to trust my intuition, I also note that I was raised to be very proud. When I look at the younger generation, I see much more humility. My generation was raised in the shadow of war. We taught that it was weak to ask for help, that it was our duty to be strong and survive on our own. I watch my children and their generation, and I see young people with the humility to question the human condition. I am so hopeful when I see young people who are prepared to be open and honest, and explore this with humility. Having said this, I haven't always witnessed this in the more rural areas of Cyprus where people of my children's generation were often raised by their grandparents. In such cases, their attitudes almost seem a generation behind; they seem prouder and repressed than many of their more cosmopolitan contemporaries.

I was raised to be proud, to be courageous and self-sufficient, and to hide any weakness. The great irony is that it actually takes a lot more courage to reveal our fears and flaws, to admit we are weak and confused, and say; "Help! I'm drowning!" Again, I think I learnt to do this—finally—by watching my children. But I was also given guidance from one very special source.

The following story always brings tears to my eyes whenever I think about it, and I have left it to the very end of this book to tell it because I somehow feel it explains everything. It's the story of the moment I was visited by an Earthly Angel, who told me everything I needed to hear and changed the course of my life forever.

A few weeks after the daily early morning marathon walks, during which I saw the blessed light that made me turn a huge corner, and after I started working with the healer, I had a visit, out of the blue, from an old friend called Irene, which I hadn't seen for years. Irene and I had met when I first moved to Cyprus in 1983. She worked in the bank where I was a customer and we struck up a friendship. Unfortunately, her husband wasn't really the sociable type, and once they started a family and she gave up work, I rarely saw her. Occasionally, we would bump into each other in the supermarket and we would always exchange pleasantries, but we were both busy with our own families and our promises of meeting for coffee dates never materialised. I had certainly not seen her since my husband died, so when she turned up at my house, several years after this tragic event, I was shocked, but pleasantly surprised.

Irene wasn't alone. She had brought a friend with her. I don't remember this woman's name, but I know she was from Switzerland. Let's call her Greta. Irene apologised for not calling on me sooner when she was all too aware of what had happened. I assured her there was nothing to apologise for. I told her I knew what it felt like to be unsure of what to do or say to someone who has experienced such a huge tragedy.

I invited Irene and Greta into my house and served them some coffee. Straight away, Greta started to tell me her life story and, despite the fog I was living in at that time, I remember her story in precise detail to this day. I am sure the fact that she was a German speaker, and thus told me her story in my own mother tongue, also made it more real and vibrant to me.

Greta explained that she had been a professional dancer in Switzerland. She was also married to her dancing partner. Together they had enjoyed a long and successful career. However, when Greta was in her mid-30s, she was involved in a serious car accident that put her in a coma for three months. When she came out of the coma, Greta discovered that both her hips had been replaced and her legs were seriously damaged. She was told that it was likely she would spend the rest of her life on crutches. A few months later, her husband left her for another dancer, his new dancing partner, and the woman who went on to become his new wife. Greta was utterly heartbroken, but she was determined to recover. She said she prayed for help, that she reached deep into a place inside her she didn't even know existed, in order to find the strength to fight, and that the only thing that kept her going was faith, the strongest faith that she would eventually recover. Already I anticipated a happy ending to this story as I could plainly see that this woman wasn't using crutches and had walked into my house as if her body was in perfect condition.

At a certain point in her rehabilitation, Greta had tried kinesiology, and it was this treatment that really put her on the right road to recovery. Within a few years, she could walk without the aid of crutches. She was so inspired that she decided to dedicate her life to studying kinesiology, and thus began a whole new career. By the time I met her, Greta was walking normally again and had started her own kinesiology practice; she had helped many people recover beyond the expectations of their doctors and was truly passionate about helping others. The faith she found had stayed with her through her rehabilitation, making her believe that there was a purpose to her journey. I was humbled by her story. I realised I had always had some faith, but maybe now I needed more. Also, I felt so grateful that I still had such a strong body. If this woman could overcome her grief and despair when she was physically so weak, simply through finding enough faith, then surely so could I. In that moment, I made a promise to myself. I pledged that I would deepen my faith, and that I would keep the firm believe that I would recover from my despair, and eventually discover the reason for why I had gone through it.

I was so moved by Greta's passion and dedication, by her strength and faith, but most of all by the fact that what had happened to her seemed so much worse than what had happened to me. She had come close to death, she had been betrayed by her love, she had seen her beloved career come to abrupt end, and she had been left with nothing but a broken body, an aching heart and a pessimistic diagnosis. At a moment when she had no one and nothing, she had reached out and found the faith to keep going. She had risen above it all, defied the doctors, mustered up the will to go on, and had been rewarded with a new, fulfilling life. It all brought tears to my eyes.

The most important thing Greta told me was that we all have spiritual helpers; that they surround us all the time and are with us from the day we are born until the day we die. We need to trust that they are there and ask them for help, otherwise they won't interfere with our lives. She said it's their divine order not to help unless we ask for it, through prayer. She advised me to pray to my spiritual helpers and stay connected to them through meditation. She also told me that whenever she feels their help, she simply lights a candle to thank them. I lit a candle as soon as Greta left my house. I couldn't have been more grateful to my spiritual helper for arranging this blessed meeting.

I never saw Greta again. In my mind, I call her my "Swiss Angel" because it really did feel like a one-off visit from an Earthly Angel. I remember hanging on her every word as she told her story, and the details remained in my mind, vividly, from that day forward. Her voice was so gentle and loving; I can still hear it in my head. I know she was one of my spiritual helpers. I trusted her. From that day forward, I thought about Greta's story whenever I needed inspiration to carry on, it helped me to stay grateful for what I had and encouraged me to have faith that there is always light at the end of the tunnel, even when we can't see it. Specifically, what Greta had told me was that, at her most desperate moment, she had simply prayed for help. She soon found that small things started happening that steered her in the right direction and enabled her to keep the faith that she would recover. Her faith gave her the will power to succeed. But the greatest message I received from Greta's story was the understanding that everything happens for a reason. If she hadn't suffered the fate she had suffered, which led her to discover her passion and skill for kinesiology, she wouldn't have been able to help all the people whose lives she had changed up to that point. After meeting Greta, as I went about my life, and continued to struggle through my own battles—small and large—one thing always kept me going, the belief that everything I was experiencing was happening for a reason.

So, what is the reason I went through everything I experienced? Well, I believe that I was meant to write this book for you. I believe that there is someone in the world who desperately needs to read this book, right now, someone who needs to know my story because they need help dealing with whatever they are going through in their life. I have faith that this book will give them the help and inspiration they may so dearly need.

If you are reading this book and you are struggling with a situation in your life, let me be your Earthly Angel of light. Let me help you find the faith you need to help you get through with whatever it's you are going through. Let me help you to trust that there is a reason for why you are suffering now and that you will, in time, discover the deeper meaning behind why you have suffered so much. I know you probably can't see it right now, and you may even feel anger at the notion that there is a "reason" for why you are in such pain, but please believe me, if you have patience and faith, you will come through and out the other side. You will discover the reason for why you have been through your pain, and both you and the world will be more fulfilled from this. Please, just have faith!

The author

Regina Ioannou-Knapp was born in 1952 in Austria. In 1970, her journey led her to Paris where she studied Psychology with Foreign Languages at the University of Paris III: Sorbonne la Nouvelle. In 1974, she became a professional tour leader in an international travel company and soon a world traveler. In 1983, she was sent for a short mission to Cyprus where she met her late husband. Together they had five children and lived an enviable life, until February 2002 when her husband suddenly passed away. She became a widow, a single mother raising her five young children, a stranger living in a foreign land trying to cope with the male-dominated society. From 1994 until 2015, she was an entrepreneur. In 2015, she wrote her first book titled "The Reason". Regina is the founder of the Institute of Motherhood and speaks on national and international events, while also working as a Life Counselor helping people find their feet back in life.

Regina currently lives in Paphos, Cyprus. Her contact details are:
Regina Ioannou-Knapp,
Email: regina.ioannou@gmail.com
Website: www.reginaioannou.org

Postal address:
Regina Ioannou-Knapp
P.O.Box 62248
8062 Paphos, Cyprus

novum 📖 PUBLISHER FOR NEW AUTHORS

The publisher

He who stops getting better stops being good.

This is the motto of novum publishing, and our focus is on finding new manuscripts, publishing them and offering long-term support to the authors.
Our publishing house was founded in 1997, and since then it has become THE expert for new authors and has won numerous awards.

Our editorial team will peruse each manuscript within a few weeks free of charge and without obligation.

You will find more information about
novum publishing and our books on the internet:

www.novumpublishing.com

novum 📖 PUBLISHER FOR NEW AUTHORS

Rate this book on our website!

www.novumpublishing.com

www.ingramcontent.com/pod-product-compliance
Lightning Source LLC
Chambersburg PA
CBHW020757160426
43192CB00006B/354